*All men know
that they must die.
And it is important that we should
understand the reasons and causes
of our exposure to the vicissitudes
of life and of death,
and the designs and purposes
of God in our coming into the world,
our sufferings here,
and our departure hence.
What is the object of
our coming into existence,
then dying and falling away,
to be here no more?
It is but reasonable
to suppose that God would reveal
something in reference to the matter,
and it is a subject we
ought to study more than any other.
We ought to study it day and night,
for the world is ignorant
in reference to their
true condition and relation.
If we have any claim on our
Heavenly Father for anything,
it is for knowledge
on this important subject.*

Joseph Smith
History of the Church 6:50

Understanding Death

Brent A. Barlow

Deseret Book Company
Salt Lake City, Utah
1979

First printing August 1979
Second printing November 1983

Library of Congress Cataloging in Publication Data
Main entry under title:
Understanding death.

   Includes bibliographical references and index.
   1.   Death—Addresses, essays, lectures.   I.   Barlow,
Brent A., 1941-
BT825.U5   236'.1   79-16414
ISBN 0-87747-781-7

Contents

Preface

"Death of a loved one is the most severe test that you will ever face, and if you can rise above your griefs and if you will trust in God, then you will be able to surmount any other difficulty with which you may be faced." (Harold B. Lee, *Ye Are the Light of the World*, Deseret Book, 1974, p. 257.)

Few subjects have created greater interest in recent years than that of death and dying. In the United States in 1970 there were no more than twenty courses taught on this subject at the college and university level; by 1974, just four years later, more than eleven hundred courses were being taught. Though the emphasis has been at the college level, formal death education now exists in junior and senior high school classes; there are even classes on the subject in many preschools and elementary schools.

While there is much that is praiseworthy being taught outside The Church of Jesus Christ of Latter-day Saints on death and dying, with this topic, as with others, we as Latter-day Saints must look within our own teachings to find that which is unique to our own denomination. This is particularly true where the Lord has given revelation. We have much in common with other religious groups, but we also have much that is unique. And since we believe in divine revelation, we have additional insights and truths on this subject. The Prophet Joseph Smith noted, "It is but reasonable to suppose that God would reveal something in reference to the matter . . . for the world is ignorant in reference to their true condition and relation. If we have any claim on our Heavenly Father for anything, it is for knowledge on this important subject." (*History of the Church* 6:50.)

The Prophet taught not only that our Heavenly Father would give us knowledge on death and dying, but indicated also that seeking such information should be given high priority. "It is a subject," he said, "we ought to study more than any other. We ought to study it day and night." (Ibid.)

My own experience with death education came a few years ago when I was teaching at the University of Wisconsin–Stout and was asked to teach a course on death and the family. Like most people, I was apprehensive about death, since the subject was seldom discussed as I was growing up. After accepting the assignment to teach the course, however, I found some of my most meaningful teaching experiences in the class during that semester. Though most of my students were either Lutherans or Catholics, I found that we had much in common. The event of death seems to have a disruptive impact on most individuals and families, regardless of religious orientation, social class, or background. Few experiences in life evoke more emotion than the event or subject of death.

If the death of a loved one is the most severe trial that an individual and perhaps a family can undergo in life, then studying and learning about death, its consequences, and how to rise above grief ought to be an integral part of family life studies. Though it is difficult, all must eventually confront the simple reality taught by Paul—"as in Adam all die . . ." (1 Corinthians 15:22). So the beginning of death education came for me as I encountered this fact of life with my students.

As I taught the class, I began to look more closely at my own religious orientation and philosophy about death and dying. My interest was heightened when my mother, Ruth Peterson Barlow, died in December 1976. Up to that time most of my involvement with death had been on the academic and cognitive level. After her death, I gained some valuable insights into the emotional or affective area of losing a loved one through death.

In the fall of 1977, I had the opportunity of going to

Brigham Young University to teach courses on marriage and the family. Shortly thereafter I proposed and taught a course titled "Death and the Latter-day Saint Family." While teaching this course I became even more aware that there was a need for a compilation of readings on the subject of death that would be oriented to the Latter-day Saint. While many fine sermons have been delivered and excellent articles written on the subject, no one volume articulates concisely some of the more pertinent LDS thought, doctrines, and philosophy on death and dying. This book is an attempt to partially fill that void.

Latter-day Saint scriptures and writings contain many important truths on death and its consequence. Section 76 of the Doctrine and Covenants is paramount in discussing life after death, and section 101 teaches: "Wherefore, fear not even unto death; for in this world your joy is not full, but in me [Jesus Christ], your joy is full. Therefore, care not for the body, neither for the life of the body; but care for the soul, and for the life of the soul." (Vv. 36-37.) On a similar note the Prophet Joseph cautioned, "When we lose a near and dear friend, upon whom we have set our hearts, it should be a caution unto us not to set our affections too firmly upon others, knowing that they may in like manner be taken from us. Our affections should be placed upon God and His work, more intensely than upon our fellow beings." (HC 4:587.) Comparing mortality to that which awaits us after death, the Prophet stated, "When men are prepared, they are better off to go hence." (HC 6:52.)

But Latter-day Saint theology does not merely teach life after death and ignore mortal realities. We have been taught through revelation that we have social obligations to one another at the time of death. By divine decree the Lord has said, "Thou shalt live together in love, insomuch that thou shalt weep for the loss of them that die." (D&C 42:45.) And not all Latter-day Saints may be aware that part of our baptismal covenants include assisting others at the time of death. Alma was able to baptize at the waters of Mormon because the candidates were "willing to bear one another's burdens, that they may be light; Yea, and are willing to mourn with those that mourn; yea, and comfort those that stand in need of comfort." (Mosiah 18:8-9.) Even more specifically, James declared that "pure religion and undefiled before God and the Father is this, To visit the fatherless and widows in their affliction." (James 1:27.) Amulek, in the Book of Mormon, put the emphasis on mortality when he stated, "For behold, this life is the time for men to prepare to meet God; yea, behold the day of this life is the day for men to perform their labors." (Alma 34:32.)

Another dimension of the teachings of the Church is that of confronting the reality of our own death. Elizabeth Kubler-Ross noted that many people think of death as something that happens "to thee and thee but not to me," and perhaps some of us are in this category. Alma the younger posed the disquieting question, "Could ye say, if ye were called to die at this time, within yourselves, that ye have been sufficiently humble?" (Alma 5:27.) Perhaps we too are like the rich fool of whom the Savior spoke in his parable: ". . . this night thy soul shall be required of thee: then whose shall those things be, which thou hast provided?" (Luke 12:20.) James posed the question "For what is your life?" and then answered: "It is even a vapour, that appeareth for a little time, and then vanisheth away." (James 4:14.)

At the funeral of Lorenzo D. Barnes, the Prophet Joseph stated: "This has been a warning voice to us all to be sober and diligent and lay aside mirth, vanity and folly, and to be prepared to die tomorrow." (HC 5:363.) And in speaking of the joys of the resurrection, he said, "And may we contemplate these things so? Yes, if we learn how to live and how to die." (HC 5:361.)

Most Latter-day Saints have developed a comprehensive philosophy about life after death, but some of us may not have a concrete philosophy about life before death. What do we desire to do? What do we want to accomplish? If our philosophy about life before death does not include the event of our own death, perhaps our philosophy is not yet complete.

The realities are: (1) Each of us is mortal and will die; (2) death is yet in the future, whether it be tomorrow or in several decades; and (3) we each have time yet in life to make decisions and, as Amulek indicated, to perform our labors. Perhaps each of us could say with Orville E. Kelley, cancer patient and founder of Make Today Count, "I do not look upon each day as another day closer to death, but as another day of life, to be appreciated and enjoyed." On a similar note, it was Henry David Thoreau who went to the woods of Walden "because I wished to live deliberately, to front only the essential facts of life, and see if I could not learn what it had to teach, and not, when I came to die, discover that I had not lived. I did not wish to live what was not life, living is so dear." (*Walden*, 2.)

In formulating my own ideas about death, I have arrived at this simple philosophy: We study death to more fully appreciate and experience life. Toward this goal this book of readings is dedicated.

There are many persons who should be acknowledged for assisting with the publication of this book of readings:

My students at both the University of Wisconsin–Stout and Brigham Young University, who have convinced me that the study of death can, indeed, enhance life.

Denise Skinner, a colleague at the University of Wisconsin–Stout, who assisted in my initial endeavors to teach about death.

Dr. J. Joel Moss, chairman of the Department of Child Development and Family Relationships, Brigham Young University, who gave encouragement and support for the project.

Verlene Haws and the CDFR secretarial staff, who assisted in typing and editing the manuscript.

Craig Smith and Gregory McKinnon, graduate students at Brigham Young University, who assisted me.

Lowell M. Durham, Jr., Eleanor Knowles, and Ralph Reynolds of Deseret Book.

My wife, Susan, and our children, who were patient while Dad worked on the book.

And finally, the numerous authors, many of whom are General Authorities, who have previously given much thought and attention to writing and speaking about death and dying.

Section 1

The
Meaning
of
Death

Tragedy or Destiny?

President Spencer W. Kimball

The daily newspaper screamed the headlines: "Plane Crash Kills 43. No Survivors of Mountain Tragedy," and thousands of voices joined in a chorus: "Why did the Lord let this terrible thing happen?"

Two automobiles crashed when one went through a red light, and six people were killed. Why would God not prevent this?

Why should a young mother die of cancer and leave her eight children motherless? Why did not the Lord heal her?

A little child was drowned; another was run over. Why?

A man died one day suddenly of a coronary occlusion as he climbed a stairway. His body was found slumped on the floor. His wife cried out in agony, "Why? Why would the Lord do this to me? Could he not have considered my three little children who still need a father?"

A young man died in the mission field and people critically questioned: "Why did not the Lord protect this youth while he was doing proselyting work?"

I wish I could answer these questions with authority, but I cannot. I am sure that sometime we'll understand and be reconciled. But for the present we must seek understanding as best we can in the gospel principles.

Was it the Lord who directed the plane into the mountain to snuff out the lives of its occupants, or were there mechanical faults or human errors?

Did our Father in heaven cause the collision of the cars

From the booklet *Tragedy or Destiny?* (Deseret Book Co., 1977). Originally printed in *Improvement Era*, March 1966, pp. 178ff.

that took six people into eternity, or was it the error of the driver who ignored safety rules?

Did God take the life of the young mother or prompt the child to toddle into the canal or guide the other child into the path of the oncoming car?

Did the Lord cause the man to suffer a heart attack? Was the death of the missionary untimely?

Answer, if you can. I cannot, for though I know God has a major role in our lives, I do not know how much he causes to happen and how much he merely permits. Whatever the answer to this question, there is another I feel sure about.

Could the Lord have prevented these tragedies? The answer is, Yes. The Lord is omnipotent, with all power to control our lives, save us pain, prevent all accidents, drive all planes and cars, feed us, protect us, save us from labor, effort, sickness, even from death, if he will. But he will not.

We should be able to understand this, because we can realize how unwise it would be for us to shield our children from all effort, from disappointments, temptations, sorrows, and suffering.

The basic gospel law is free agency and eternal development. To force us to be careful or righteous would be to nullify that fundamental law and make growth impossible.

"And the Lord spake unto Adam, saying: Inasmuch as thy children are conceived in sin, even so when they begin to grow up, sin conceiveth in their hearts, and they taste the bitter, that they may know to prize the good. And it is given unto them to know good from evil; wherefore they are agents unto themselves. . . ." (Moses 6:55-56.) ". . . Satan rebelled against me, and sought to destroy the agency of man, which I, the Lord God, had given him. . . ." (Moses 4:3.)

If we looked at mortality as the whole of existence, then pain, sorrow, failure, and short life would be calamity. But if we look upon life as an eternal thing stretching far into the pre-earth past and on into the eternal post-death future, then all happenings may be put in perspective.

Is there not wisdom in his giving us trials that we might rise above them, responsibilities that we might achieve, work to harden our muscles, sorrows to try our souls? Are we not exposed to temptations to test our strength, sickness that we might learn patience, death that we might be immortalized and glorified?

If all the sick for whom we pray were healed, if all the righteous were protected and the wicked destroyed, the whole program of the Father would be annulled and the basic principle of the gospel, free agency, would be ended. No man would have to live by faith.

If joy and peace and rewards were instantaneously given the doer of good, there could be no evil—all would do good but not because of the rightness of doing good. There would be no test of strength, no development of character, no growth of powers, no free agency, only satanic controls.

Should all prayers be immediately answered according to our selfish desires and our limited understanding, then there would be little or no suffering, sorrow, disappointment, or even death, and if these were not, there would also be no joy, success, resurrection, eternal life, or godhood. "For it must needs be, that there is an opposition in all things . . . righteousness . . . wickedness . . . holiness . . . misery . . . good . . . bad. . . ." (2 Nephi 2:11.)

Being human, we would expel from our lives physical pain and mental anguish and assure ourselves of continual ease and comfort, but if we were to close the doors upon sorrow and distress, we might be excluding our greatest friends and benefactors. Suffering can make saints of people as they learn patience, long-suffering, and self-mastery. The sufferings of our Savior were part of his education. "Though he were a Son, yet learned he obedience by the things which he suffered; And being made perfect, he became the author of eternal salvation unto all them that obey him." (Hebrews 5:8-9.)

I love the verse of "How Firm a Foundation"—

> *When through the deep waters I call thee to go,*
> *The rivers of sorrow shall not thee o'erflow*
> *For I will be with thee, thy troubles to bless,*
> *And sanctify to thee thy deepest distress.*
>
> —*Hymns,* no. 66

Elder James E. Talmage wrote: "No pang that is suffered by man or woman upon the earth will be without its compensating effect . . . if it be met with patience."

On the other hand, these things can crush us with their mighty impact if we yield to weakness, complaining, and criticism.

"No pain that we suffer, no trial that we experience is wasted. It ministers to our education, to the development of such qualities as patience, faith, fortitude and humility. All that we suffer and all that we endure, especially when we endure it patiently, builds up our characters, purifies our hearts, expands our souls, and makes us more tender and charitable, more worthy to be called the children of God . . . and it is through sorrow and suffering, toil and tribulation, that we gain the education that we come here to acquire and which will make us more like our Father and Mother in heaven. . . ." (Orson F. Whitney.)

There are people who are bitter as they watch loved ones suffer agonies and interminable pain and physical torture. Some would charge the Lord with unkindness, indifference, and injustice. We are so incompetent to judge!

I like also the words of these verses, the author of which I do not know:

Pain stayed so long I said to him today,
"I will not have you with me any more."

I stamped my foot and said, "Be on your way,"
And paused there, startled at the look he wore.

"I, who have been your friend," he said to me,
"I, who have been your teacher—all you know
Of understanding love, of sympathy,
And patience, I have taught you. Shall I go?"

He spoke the truth, this strange unwelcome guest;
I watched him leave, and knew that he was wise.

He left a heart grown tender in my breast.

He left a far, clear vision in my eyes.

I dried my tears, and lifted up a song—
Even for one who'd tortured me so long.

The power of the priesthood is limitless, but God has wisely placed upon each of us certain limitations. I may develop priesthood power as I perfect my life, yet I am grateful that even through the priesthood I cannot heal all the sick. I might heal people who should die. I might relieve people of suffering who should suffer. I fear I would frustrate the purposes of God.

Had I limitless power, and yet limited vision and understanding, I might have saved Abinadi from the flames of fire when he was burned at the stake, and in doing so I might have irreparably damaged him. He died a martyr and went to a martyr's reward—exaltation.

I would likely have protected Paul against his woes if my power were boundless. I would surely have healed his "thorn in the flesh." And in doing so I might have foiled the Lord's program. Thrice Paul offered prayers, asking the Lord to remove the "thorn" from him, but the Lord did not so answer his prayers. Paul many times could have lost himself if he had been eloquent, well, handsome, and free from the things that made him humble. He speaks:

"And lest I should be exalted above measure through the abundance of the revelations, there was given to me a thorn in the flesh, the messenger of Satan to buffet me, lest I should be exalted above measure.

"And he said unto me, My grace is sufficient for thee: for my strength is made perfect in weakness. Most gladly therefore will I rather glory in my infirmities, that the power of Christ may rest upon me.

"Therefore I take pleasure in infirmities, in reproaches, in necessities, in persecutions, in distresses for Christ's sake: for when I am weak, then am I strong." (2 Corinthians 12:7, 9-10.)

I fear that had I been in Carthage Jail on June 27, 1844, I might have deflected the bullets that pierced the body of the Prophet and the Patriarch. I might have saved them from the sufferings and agony, but lost to them the martyr's death and reward. I am glad I did not have to make that decision.

With such uncontrolled power, I surely would have felt to protect Christ from the agony in Gethsemane, the insults, the thorny crown, the indignities in the court, the physical injuries. I would have administered to his wounds and healed them, giving him cooling water instead of vinegar. I might have saved him from suffering and death, and lost to the world his atoning sacrifice.

I would not dare to take the responsibility of bringing back to life my loved ones. Christ himself acknowledged the difference between his will and the Father's when he prayed that the cup of suffering be taken from him; yet he added, "Nevertheless, not my will but thine be done."

For the one who dies, life goes on and his free agency continues; and death, which seems to us such a calamity, could be a blessing in disguise just as well for one who is not a martyr.

Melvin J. Ballard wrote: "I lost a son six years of age and I saw him a man in the spirit world after his death, and I saw how he had exercised his own freedom of choice and would obtain of his own will and volition a companionship, and in due time to him and all those who are worthy of it, shall come all of the blessings and sealing privileges of the house of the Lord. . . ." (*Three Degrees of Glory.*)

If we say that early death is a calamity, disaster, or tragedy, would it not be saying that mortality is preferable to earlier entrance into the spirit world and to eventual salvation and exaltation? If mortality be the perfect state, then death would be a frustration, but the gospel teaches us there is no tragedy in death, but only in sin. ". . . blessed are the dead that die in the Lord. . . ." (D&C 63:49.)

We know so little. Our judgment is so limited. We judge the Lord's ways from our own narrow view.

I spoke at the funeral service of a young Brigham Young University student who died during World War II. There had been hundreds of thousands of young men rushed prematurely into eternity through the ravages of that war, and I made the statement that I believed this righteous youth had been called to the spirit world to preach the gospel to these deprived souls. This may not be true of all who die, but I felt it true of him.

In his vision of "The Redemption of the Dead" President Joseph F. Smith saw this very thing. He sat studying the scriptures on October 3, 1918, particularly the statements in Peter's epistle regarding the antediluvians. He writes:

"As I pondered over these things which are written, the eyes of my understanding were opened, and the Spirit of the Lord rested upon me, and I saw the hosts of the dead. . . .

"While this vast multitude of the righteous waited and conversed, rejoicing in the hour of their deliverance . . . the Son of God appeared, declaring liberty to the captives who had been faithful;

"And there he preached to them the . . . redemption of mankind from the fall, and from individual sins on conditions of repentance.

"But unto the wicked he did not go, and among the ungodly and the unrepentant who had defiled themselves while in the flesh, his voice was not raised;

"Neither did the rebellious who rejected the testimonies and the warnings of the ancient prophets behold his presence, nor look upon his face. . . .

"And as I wondered, . . . I perceived that the Lord went not in person among the wicked and the disobedient who had rejected the truth . . .

"But behold, from among the righteous he organized his forces . . . and commissioned them to go forth and carry the light of the gospel. . . .

". . . our Redeemer spent his time . . . in the world of spirits, instructing and preparing the faithful spirits . . . who had testified of him in the flesh;

"That they might carry the message of redemption unto all the dead, unto whom he could not go personally, because of their rebellion and transgression. . . .

"Among the great and mighty ones who were assembled in this vast congregation of the righteous were Father Adam . . . Eve, with many of her faithful daughters . . . Abel, the first martyr, . . . Seth, . . . Noah, . . . Shem, the great High Priest; Abraham, . . . Isaac, Jacob, and Moses . . . Ezekiel, . . . Daniel. . . .

"All these and many more, even the prophets who dwelt among the Nephites. . . .

"The Prophet Joseph Smith, and my father, Hyrum Smith, Brigham Young, . . . and other choice spirits . . . in the spirit world.

"I observed that they were also among the noble and great ones who were chosen in the beginning to be rulers in the Church of God. . . .

"I beheld that the faithful elders of this dispensation, when they depart from mortal life, continue their labors in the preaching of the gospel of repentance and redemption. . . ." (D&C 138.)

Death, then, may be the opening of the door to opportunities, including that of teaching the gospel of Christ. There is no greater work.

Despite the fact that death opens new doors, we do not seek it. We are admonished to pray for those who are ill and use our priesthood power to heal them.

"And the elders of the church, two or more, shall be called, and shall pray for and lay their hands upon them in my name; and if they die they shall die unto me, and if they live they shall live unto me.

"Thou shalt live together in love, insomuch that thou shalt weep for the loss of them that die, and more especially for those that have not hope of a glorious resurrection.

"And it shall come to pass that those that die in me shall not taste of death, for it shall be sweet unto them;

"And they that die not in me, wo unto them, for their death is bitter.

"And again, it shall come to pass that he that hath faith in me to be healed, and is not appointed unto death, shall be healed." (D&C 42:44-48.)

We are assured by the Lord that the sick will be healed if the ordinance is performed, if there is sufficient faith, and if the ill one is "not appointed unto death." All of these three factors should be satisfied. Many do not comply with the ordinances, and great numbers are unwilling or incapable of exercising sufficient faith. But the third factor also looms important: if they are not appointed unto death.

Everyone must die. Death is an important part of life. Of course, we are never quite ready for the change. Not knowing when it will come, we properly fight to retain our life. Yet we ought not be afraid of death. We pray for the sick, we administer to the afflicted, and we implore the Lord to heal and reduce pain, save life, and postpone death, and properly so, but not because eternity is so frightful.

The Prophet Joseph Smith confirmed: "The Lord takes many away even in infancy, that they may escape the envy of man, and the sorrows and evils of this present world; they were too pure, too lovely, to live on this earth; therefore, if rightly considered, instead of mourning we have reason to rejoice as they are delivered from evil, and we shall have them again. . . . The only difference between the old and the young dying is, one lives longer in heaven and eternal light and glory than the other, and is freed a little sooner from this miserable wicked world." (*Teachings of the Prophet Joseph Smith*, pp. 196-97.)

Just as Ecclesiastes (3:2) says, I am confident that there is a time to die, but I believe also that many people die before "their time" because they are careless, abuse their bodies, take unnecessary chances, or expose themselves to hazards, accidents, and sickness.

Of the antediluvians, we read: "Hast thou marked the old way which wicked men have trodden? Which were cut down out of time, whose foundation was overflown with a flood." (Job 22:15-16.)

In Ecclesiastes 7:17 we find this statement: "Be not over much wicked, neither be thou foolish: why shouldest thou die before thy time?"

I believe we may die prematurely but seldom exceed our time very much. One exception was Hezekiah, twenty-five-year-old king of Judah who was far more godly than his successors or predecessors: "In those days was Hezekiah sick unto death. And the prophet Isaiah . . . came to him, and said unto him, Thus saith the Lord, Set thine house in order; for thou shalt die, and not live."

Hezekiah, loving life as we do, turned his face to the wall and wept bitterly, saying: ". . . remember now how I have walked before thee in truth and with a perfect heart, and have done that which is good in thy sight. . . ." The Lord yielded unto his prayers. "I have heard thy prayer, I have seen thy tears: behold, I will heal thee: . . . And I will add unto thy days fifteen years; and I will deliver thee and this city out of the hand of the king of Assyria. . . ." (2 Kings 20:1, 3, 5-6.)

A modern illustration of this exceptional extension of life took place in November 1881.

My uncle, David Patten Kimball, left his home in Arizona on a trip across the Salt River desert. He had fixed up his books and settled accounts and had told his wife of a premonition that he would not return. He was lost on the desert for two days and three nights, suffering untold agonies of thirst and pain. He passed into the spirit world and described later, in a letter of January 8, 1882, to his sister, what happened there. He had seen his parents. "My father . . . told me I could remain there if I chose to do so, but I pleaded with him that I might stay with my family long enough to make them comfortable, to repent of my sins, and more fully prepare myself for the change. Had it not been for this, I never should have returned home, except as a corpse. Father finally told me I could remain two years and to do all the good I could during that time, after which he would come for me. . . . He mentioned four others that he would come for also. . . ."

Two years to the day from that experience on the desert he died easily and apparently without pain. Shortly before he died he looked up and called, "Father, Father." Within approximately a year of his death the other four men named were also dead.

God has many times preserved the lives of his servants until they could complete their work—Abinadi, Enoch, the sons of Helaman, and Paul.

And God will sometimes use his power over death to protect us. Heber C. Kimball was subjected to a test that, like the one given Abraham, was well-nigh unthinkable. Comfortless and in great perplexity, he importuned the Prophet Joseph to inquire of the Lord, and the Prophet received this revelation: "Tell him to go and do as he has been commanded, and if I see that there is any danger of his apostatizing, I will take him to myself." (Orson F. Whitney, *Life of Heber C. Kimball.*)

God controls our lives, guides and blesses us, but gives us our agency. We may live our lives in accordance with his plan for us or we may foolishly shorten or terminate them.

I am positive in my mind that the Lord has planned our destiny. Sometime we'll understand fully, and when we see back from the vantage point of the future, we shall be satisfied with many of the happenings of this life that are so difficult for us to comprehend.

We sometimes think we would like to know what lies ahead, but sober thought brings us back to accepting life a day at a time and magnifying and glorifying that day. Sister Ida Allredge gave us a thought-provoking verse:

*I cannot know the future, nor the path I shall have
    trod,*
*But by that inward vision, which points the way to
    God.*

*I would not glimpse the beauty or joy for me in
    store,*
*Lest patience ne'er restrain me from thrusting wide
    the door.*

I would not part the curtains or cast aside the veil,
*Else sorrows that await me might make my courage
    fail;*
*I'd rather live not knowing, just doing my small
    mite;*
*I'd rather walk by faith with God, than try alone the
    light.*

We knew before we were born that we were coming to the earth for bodies and experience and that we would have joys and sorrows, ease and pain, comforts and hardships, health and sickness, successes and disappointments. We knew also that after a period of life we would die. We accepted all these eventualities with a glad heart, eager to accept both the favorable and the unfavorable. We eagerly accepted the chance to come earthward even though it might be for only a day or a year. Perhaps we were not so much concerned whether we should die of disease, of acci-

dent, or of senility. We were willing to take life as it came
and as we might organize and control it, and this
without murmur, complaint, or unreasonable demands.

In the face of apparent tragedy we must put our trust in
God, knowing that despite our limited view, his purposes
will not fail. With all its troubles, life offers us the tremendous privilege to grow in knowledge and wisdom, faith and
works, preparing to return and share God's glory.

From the Valley of Despair to the Mountain Peaks of Hope

President Harold B. Lee

This is to me a most significant occasion° and a most difficult assignment about which I have prayed most earnestly that I might have the proper spirit and inspiration. The purpose of this service is not to glorify war, but, from the Lord's own declaration, to set forth clearly the position of the Church with regard to war. We do not wish to enter into a controversy as to the rightness or wrongness of war, but to set at rest the torments of those who have loved ones engaged in the ugly conflicts of war. We are not here to open old wounds in hearts that have been torn with the devastation which comes with the sense of loneliness because of the loss of loved ones.

We are here to help lift the eyes of those who mourn from the valley of despair to the light upon the mountain peaks of hope, to endeavor to answer questions about war, to bring peace to troubled souls, not as the world giveth, but only that which comes from the Prince of Peace. We are here to lift all of us out of the shadows into life and light.

In our generation the true Christian's position on war is clearly set forth by a declaration in which the Lord says, "Therefore, renounce war and proclaim peace. . . ." (D&C 98:16.)

What is the position of the Church with respect to war? A declaration of the First Presidency given during World

---

°Note: This address was delivered at a special Memorial Day service, May 30, 1971. It has been printed in Harold B. Lee, *Ye Are the Light of the World* (Deseret Book Co., 1974), pp. 251-60.

War II is still applicable in our time. The statement said:
". . . the Church is and must be against war. The Church
itself cannot wage war unless and until the Lord shall issue
new commands. It cannot regard war as a righteous means
of settling international disputes; these should and could be
settled—the nations agreeing—by peaceful negotiations
and adjustments."

There is a scripture that has direct bearing here:

"And now, verily I say unto you concerning the laws of
the land, it is my will that my people should observe to do
all things whatsoever I command them.

"And that law of the land which is constitutional, supporting that principle of freedom in maintaining rights and
privileges, belongs to all mankind, and is justifiable before
me.

"Therefore, I, the Lord, justify you, and your brethren
of my church, in befriending that law which is the constitutional law of the land;

"And as pertaining to the law of man, whatsoever is
more or less than this, cometh of evil." (D&C 98:4-7.)

Note particularly that the revelation is directed to
members of the Church. Therefore, it is applicable to persons of all nations, not only those in America.

There are many who are troubled and their souls har-
rowed by the haunting question of the position of the
soldier who in combat kills the enemy. Again, the First
Presidency has commented: "When, therefore, constitutional law, obedient to those principles, calls the manhood
of the Church into the armed service of any country to
which they owe allegiance, their highest civic duty requires
that they meet that call. If, hearkening to that call and
obeying those in command over them, they shall take the
lives of those who fight against them, that will not make of
them murderers, nor subject them to the penalty that God
has prescribed for those who kill, beyond the principles to
be mentioned shortly: for it would be a cruel God that
would punish his children as moral sinners for acts done by
them as the innocent instrumentalities of a sovereign whom
he had told them to obey and whose will they were power-
less to resist."

God is at the helm.

I will paraphrase the next statement from the message of the First Presidency in order to make these words more applicable today. The whole world seems presently to be in commotion. As the Lord foretold, we are in a time when men's hearts fail them. There are many persons who are engaged in wars who are devout Christians. They are innocent instrumentalities—war instrumentalities, for the most part—of their warring sovereignties. On each side, people believe that they are fighting for a just cause, for defense of home and country and freedom. On each side they pray to the same God, in the same name, for victory. Both sides cannot be wholly right; perhaps neither is without wrong. God will work out in his own due time and in his own sovereign way the justice and right of the conflict. But he will not hold the innocent instrumentalities of the war—our brethren in arms—responsible for the conflict.

Another question often asked is, Why was not my son or brother or husband or fiance protected on the fields of battle as were others who testify that they were miraculously spared? People who have lost their loved ones are ofttimes troubled by faith-promoting incidents of those who have been miraculously spared. They may say, "Why did it have to happen to my boy (or my husband or my brother or my fiance)?"

While this question may never be fully answered in this life, we are given some illuminating observations from sacred writings. Eternal law does apply to war and those who engage in it. This law was declared by the Master Himself when Peter struck off the ear of Malchus, who was a servant of the Jewish high priest. Jesus reproved Peter, saying, "Put up again thy sword into his place: for all they that take the sword shall perish with the sword." (Matthew 26:52.)

In other words, those who are the perpetrators of war shall perish by the destructive forces that they have unloosed.

The sin, as Moroni of old said, is upon those who sit in their places of power and "in a state of thoughtless stupor" (Alma 60:7), in a frenzy of hate; who lust for unrighteous power and dominion over their fellowmen, and who have put into motion eternal forces that they do not comprehend or cannot control. In his own due time God will pass sentence upon such leaders.

Therefore, let us endeavor to banish all bitterness from our hearts and to rest judgment with God, as did the apostle Paul when he wrote, ". . . Vengeance is mine; I will repay, saith the Lord." (Romans 12:19.)

There is another question that is often asked: Why did he or she have to die? What is the purpose of life if it is to be so ruthlessly destroyed?

To the prophet Moses, the Lord answered this question in one sentence: "For behold, this is my work and my glory . . . to bring to pass the immortality and eternal life of man." (Moses 1:39.)

Immortality is a free gift to all mankind, but eternal life must be won by deeds done in the flesh.

Recently I received a letter from parents in California whose son had written home just before last Christmas and then shortly thereafter his life was taken in the war in Vietnam. This is part of what he wrote: "War is an ugly thing, a vicious thing. It makes men do things they would not normally do. It breaks up families, causes immorality, cheating, and much hatred. It is not the glorious John Wayne type thing you see in the movies. It is going a month without a shower and a change of clothing. It is fear creeping up your spine when you hear a mortar tube in the jungle. It is not being able to get close enough to the ground when coming under enemy fire; hearing your buddy cry out because of being ripped with a hot piece of shrapnel. You men be proud of your American citizenship, because many brave and valiant men are here preserving your freedom. [This letter was written to his priesthood quorum back home.] God has given you the gift of a free nation, and it is the duty of each of you to help in whatever way you can to preserve it. America is the protector of our church, which is dearer to me than life itself." And then this young man said this very significant thing: "I realize now that I have already received the greatest gift of all, and that is the opportunity to gain exaltation and eternal life. If you have this gift, nothing else really matters."

It is that hope and that faith that has sustained our Latter-day Saints in the military, both the living and the dead. This hope is declared in the scriptures: ". . . therefore this life became a probationary state; a time to prepare to meet God; a time to prepare for that endless state which has been spoken of by us, which is after the resurrection of the dead." (Alma 12:24.)

President Joseph F. Smith made an enlightening comment on this subject. He said, "Many things occur in the world in which it seems very difficult for most of us to find a solid reason for the acknowledgment of the hand of the Lord. I have come to the belief that the only reason I have been able to discover by which we should acknowledge the hand of God in some occurrences is the fact that the thing which has occurred has been permitted of the Lord." (*Gospel Doctrine*, p. 56.) It was not the will of the Lord, but it occurred by permission of the Lord.

George Washington is quoted as having said at one time, "This liberty will look easy by and by when nobody has to die to get it."

No doubt many of you fathers have said in your hearts, as did King David when the sad news of his son Absalom's death was brought to him, "O my son Absalom, my son, my son Absalom! would God I had died for thee, O Absalom, my son, my son!" (2 Samuel 18:33.)

And you mothers may have reacted as did that sainted mother of the young Royal Air Force pilot who was lost in an ill-fated flight over the North Sea. Here are the words of Sister Zina C. Brown when her young son Hugh C. was killed. This lovely wife of Elder Hugh B. Brown, our beloved associate, wrote this perhaps as she remembered the words of the Master in Gethsemane:

> *Forgive the clouding doubt that one instant*
> *hid Thy face from mine;*
> *With my face toward the light I shall walk*
> *by faith until my summons come.*
>
> *Dear Father, through Thy Son I pray, and*
> *praise Thy holy name,*

And, with full heart, made glad by
Thy redeeming love,
I humbly say, "Thy Will Be Done."

"If in this life only we have hope in Christ, we are of all men most miserable," said the Apostle Paul. (1 Corinthians 15:19.) If we fail to understand this great truth, we will be miserable in time of need, and then sometimes our faith may be challenged. But if we have a faith that looks beyond the grave and trusts in divine Providence to bring all things in their proper perspective in due time, then we have hope, and our fears are calmed. Life does not end with mortal death. Through temple ordinances which bind on earth and in heaven, every promised blessing predicated upon faithfulness will be realized.

One of our friends said to me recently, "I can't make my wife believe that the Lord always answers prayers; even when He says 'no,' He's answered our prayers."

"Let not your heart be troubled" were the first of the parting words of the Master when he said, "In my Father's house are many mansions: if it were not so, I would have told you. I go to prepare a place for you.

"And if I go and prepare a place for you, I will come again, and receive you unto myself; that where I am, there ye may be also." (John 14:1-3.)

And then he said: "Peace I leave with you, my peace I give unto you: not as the world giveth, give I unto you. Let not your heart be troubled, neither let it be afraid." (John 14:27.)

Having gone through some similar experiences in losing loved ones in death, I speak from personal experience when I say to you who mourn, do not try to live too many days ahead. The all-important thing is not that tragedies and sorrows come into our lives, but what we do with them. Death of a loved one is the most severe test that you will ever face, and if you can rise above your griefs and if you will trust in God, then you will be able to surmount any other difficulty with which you may be faced.

One of America's most gifted writers, Henry Wadsworth Longfellow, wrote of this three years after his wife had died, as he longed for her still. Time had not softened his grief nor eased the torment of his memories. He had no heart for poetry. He had no heart for anything, it seemed. Life had become an empty dream. But this could not go on, he told himself. He was letting the days slip by, nursing his despondency. Life was not an empty dream. He must be up and doing. Let the past bury its dead. Suddenly Longfellow was writing in a surge of inspiration, the lines coming almost too quickly for his racing pen. Here are three verses of this immortal and inspired message to those whom he loved:

> *Tell me not, in mournful numbers,*
> *Life is but an empty dream!—*
> *For the soul is dead that slumbers,*
> *And things are not what they seem.*

> *Life is real! Life is earnest!*
> *And the grave is not its goal;*
> *Dust thou art, to dust returnest,*
> *Was not spoken of the soul.*

> *Let us then be up and doing,*
> *With a heart for any fate;*
> *Still achieving, still pursuing,*
> *Learn to labor and to wait.*

Longfellow wrote these verses and titled his poem "The Psalm of Life." He put it aside at first, unwilling to show it to anyone. As he later explained, "It was a voice from my inmost heart, at a time when I was rallying from depression."

The immortal words of Abraham Lincoln come back for us to ponder: "With malice toward none, with charity for all, with firmness in the right as God gives us to see the right, let us strive on to finish the work we are in, to bind up the nation's wounds, to care for him who shall have borne the battle, and for his widow and his orphan, to all which may achieve a just and lasting peace among ourselves and with all nations." (Second Inaugural Address.)

The blessing to be found in pain is a right-here, right-now blessing, taking place in the very midst of suffering.

As a result of his many experiences with suffering, that great humanitarian, Dr. Albert Schweitzer, gave this advice: "Don't vex your mind by trying to explain the suffering you have to endure in this life. Don't think that God is punishing you or disciplining you or that he has rejected you. Even in the midst of your suffering, you are in his kingdom. You are always his child, and he has his protecting arms around you. Does a child understand everything his father does? No, but he can confidently nestle in his father's arms and feel perfect happiness, even while tears glisten in his eyes, because he is his father's child."

It was a wise man who said, "We cannot banish dangers, but we can banish fears. We must not demean life, by standing in awe of death."

Remember the story of Job. After his torment his wife came to him and said: "Dost thou still retain thine integrity? curse God, and die." (Job 2:9.)

And in the majesty of his faith, Job said:

"For I know that my redeemer liveth, and that he shall stand at the latter day upon the earth:

"And though after my skin worms destroy this body, yet in my flesh shall I see God:

"Whom I shall see for myself, and mine eyes shall behold, and not another; though my reins be consumed within me." (Job 19:25-27.)

So to you who have lost loved ones, to you who know the pangs of loneliness, some of us have also gone through the fire and understand what it means. We say to you that in the faith that lifts you beyond the sordid trials of the day and points you to the glorious tomorrow that can be yours, you too, like the prophet Job, can say, "I know that my Redeemer lives."

I leave you my blessing, to bring you the peace that can come only from this knowledge and from the witness that you can receive if you will put your trust in your Heavenly Father.

I know that God lives. I know that he has opened the doors to the glorious resurrection. He is biding the time when he shall come again, when the trump shall sound and those who are ready to come forth in the morning of the resurrection shall come forth to be caught up in the clouds of heaven to meet him. God grant that we may live to be worthy to be among those who will be with him.

Life . . . and Questions That Linger

Richard L. Evans

Whether young or old, at whatever age, the question of life, of its length, of its everlastingness always lingers—sometimes insistently, sometimes suppressed. But the question becomes acute when someone close to us, or someone cherished or admired or loved by us, leaves this life. And through the lingering thoughts, and sometimes shadowing of doubts, of loneliness, of deep and yearning desire, comes the renewal of assurance that life is everlasting—for ourselves, and for our loved ones—and the evidence is overwhelming for the reality of eternal continuance.

"Let us accustom ourselves," wrote Maurice Maeterlinck, "to regard death as a form of life which we do not yet understand. . . . Death is but . . . a departure into an unknown filled with wonderful promises. . . ." And as to "our future beyond the grave, it is in no way necessary that we should have an answer to everything. . . . Total annihilation is impossible. . . . Neither a body nor a thought can drop out of the universe, out of time and space . . . for there is no place where anything ceases to be. . . . To be able to do away with a thing—that is to say, to fling it into nothingness—nothingness would have to exist; and, if it exist, under whatever form, it is no longer nothingness. . . ." There is no such thing as nothingness. "There is no such thing as immaterial matter." (D&C 131:7.)

As we continue, so do loved ones, so do principles, so do

"The Spoken Word" from Temple Square, presented over KSL and the Columbia Broadcasting System March 30, 1969. Copyright 1969. Reprinted in *Improvement Era*, June 1969, p. 82.

eternal purposes. And so, as we consider life and death, and the reality of resurrection, we turn our thoughts to Him who showed the way of life and redeemed us from death. May we use this moment of time to live to realize the best of all there is of life with loved ones, through the endless opportunities of eternity.

What Is the Purpose of Suffering?

Kenneth H. Beesley

Why does a mother have to die and leave young children, or why does a person have to lose a leg, his ability to move, or his eyesight? Why does a person have to suffer from cancer? And from these questions grows another question, the real question: Why does God let it happen?

The history of the Church is replete with examples of persecution, deprivation, martyrdom, starvation, and imprisonment, as well as the quiet agonies of the soul. It is not surprising that the purpose of suffering has been discussed in every generation from Joseph Smith to our prophets today.

Revelation and the words of our Church leaders refer not to one reason for suffering but many. This may distress the young mother whose husband is killed in battle. She wants to know *the reason*, not a listing of a dozen or more alternatives. People want a personal answer. Why must *I* suffer from cancer? Why was *my* son born with limited mental capacities? Why me? How can I know? The answer in full lies only in the mind of God.

For some the greatest pain may be not knowing why they suffer. Suffering is often easier to bear when we understand its purpose. Is it a judgment from God for something I've done? If not, then why did God permit it to happen? There are some whose faith in God is tried or even shattered because they cannot reconcile the tragedies of war,

From *New Era*, April 1975, pp. 36-39.

natural disaster, or the suffering of loved ones with the goodness of God.

I do not pretend to speak for the Church, nor do I intend in any way to minimize the extent of suffering in the world or the anguish an individual may feel. And although I have sought insight from the scriptures and writings of our General Authorities, the conclusions I have reached are my own.

More important than what happens to us (or the reason why it occurs) is how we react to it.

It appears there are several reasons why suffering occurs:

1. God causes it.

2. An individual brings it on himself.

3. Someone intentionally causes another person to suffer.

4. Human error may unintentionally cause suffering.

5. An act of nature precipitates the damage, injury, or death.

6. A mechanical malfunction causes an accident.

1. *Suffering caused by God.*

There is evidence that God sometimes intervenes in the events of this world. The scriptures suggest that suffering may sometimes be a form of loving chastisement from the Lord. "As many as I love, I rebuke and chasten. . . ." (Revelation 3:19.) "Whom the Lord loveth he chasteneth. . . ." (Hebrews 12:6.) "My son, despise not the chastening of the Lord; neither be weary of his correction: For whom the Lord loveth he correcteth; even as a father the son in whom he delighteth." (Proverbs 3:11-12.)

Sufferings from the Lord are sometimes a "smiting of the wicked," but not all suffering is caused by unrighteousness. (Brigham Young, *Journal of Discourses* 13:147.)

2. *Suffering caused by our own actions.*

Human error and the violation of civil, natural, or eternal laws may frequently cause us pain. Unfortunately, it sometimes is difficult for us to understand this. Through rationalization, projection, or selective inattention, we so often excuse ourselves, blaming our self-induced problem on someone else.

3. *Sufferings caused by others.*

Saints who lived during the Missouri or Illinois periods knew what it meant to suffer at the hands of others. Driven from their homes into the bitter cold of winter, tarred and feathered, shot in cold blood—they knew well the sufferings of persecution. Less dramatic but very real suffering can be caused by an unkind word, a slight or discourtesy. A person can be hurt by an unfair or dishonest business transaction.

4. *Unintentionally produced suffering.*

Sometimes a person may bring suffering on himself or others unintentionally. Insensitivity to the feeling of others or misunderstanding of another's motives often is to blame. While such suffering may have been unintentionally produced, the discomfiture will not be unlike a pain purposely inflicted.

5. *Suffering caused by an act of nature.*

Floods, earthquakes, violent storms, or other cataclysmic occurrences in nature frequently destroy property, cause injuries, or take lives. While God has at times calmed the storms, the forces of nature are, for the most part, allowed to function unhindered. Suffering of this kind may be permitted by God since he has the power to temper the elements, but he seldom causes the suffering as a purposeful act.

6. *Suffering caused by a mechanical failure or malfunction that causes an accident.*

The car's brakes fail; the electrical wire shorts and overheats; the altimeter jams—a crash occurs, a fire flares, a plane is down, and suffering or death results. Why? Did God cause it? Was it a punishment for past sins? I think not. Danger is simply inherent in this life. Still, although God seldom causes suffering, he *does* allow it. Why?

One of the most important principles of eternity is free agency. The Book of Mormon explains that to properly exercise our agency, we need to have an opposition in all things. (See 2 Nephi 2:11.) The Lord is omnipotent and could control our lives, "save us pain; prevent all accident; drive all planes and cars; feed us; protect us; save us from labor, effort, sickness, even from death. But is that what you want? . . .

"Should we be protected from hardship, pain, suffering, sacrifice, or labor (or an accident)? Should the Lord protect the righteous? Should he immediately punish the wicked? . . . If we look at mortality as a complete existence, then pain, sorrow and a short life could be a calamity. But if we look upon the whole of life in its eternal perspective stretching far into the premortal past and into the eternal post-death future, then all happenings may have more meaning and may fall into proper place." (Spencer W. Kimball, "Tragedy or Destiny," *BYU Speeches of the Year*, 1955.)

God allows us to enter this world with all its risks, aware that facing and overcoming such perils is essential to our eternal progression. You recall that Joseph Smith while in Liberty Jail pleaded with the Lord concerning his own sufferings and those of his fellow Saints. The Lord answered, "If thou art called to pass through tribulation; if thou art in perils among false brethren; if thou art in perils among robbers; if thou art in perils by land or by sea; . . . if the billowing surge conspire against thee; if fierce winds become thine enemy; . . . if the very jaws of hell shall gape open the mouth wide after thee, know thou, my son, that *all these things shall give thee experience, and shall be for thy good."* (D&C 122: 5, 7. Italics added.)

What seems to be a tragedy (and a cause for suffering) may from an eternal perspective be a blessing and a cause for rejoicing. Sufferings have the potential of blessing man. They may strengthen us for future tasks. They can make us sensitive to the pains of others and more willing to sacrifice for others. (Christ suggests that one must lose his life to find it.) They may help us appreciate Christ's atonement; they may help to purge our imperfections and to purify us.

Suffering may be a "school" of experience, and present impediments may ultimately be seen as a part of our life's foundation.

Elder Orson F. Whitney wrote: "No pain that we suffer, no trial that we experience is wasted. It ministers to our education, to the development of such qualities as patience, faith, fortitude, and humility. All that we suffer . . . builds up our characters, purifies our hearts, expands our souls, and makes us more tender and charitable, more worthy to be called the children of God . . . and it is through sorrow and suffering, toil and tribulation, that we gain the education which will make us more like our Father and Mother in heaven."

Obedience may be learned from suffering. "Though he were a Son [speaking of Christ], yet learned he obedience by the things which he suffered." (Hebrews 5:8.)

Superior blessings from God are dependent upon our being severely tried and tested. Suffering may lead us to put our trust in the Lord and to keep his commandments. Of course, Alma suggests we can learn obedience without first being humbled by experiences, but many of us need help.

Bitter sufferings are necessary for us to experience sweet enjoyment.

Without trials, we tend to forget the Lord, as the Book of Mormon makes clear. However, God's spirit is manifest abundantly to those who are faithful under trials.

Paul's "thorn in the flesh" and other tribulations were a pleasure to him. "Therefore I take pleasure in infirmities, in reproaches, in necessities, in persecutions, in distresses for Christ's sake: for when I am weak, then am I strong." (2 Corinthians 12:10.)

Our present adversities may have immediate value as well as preparing us for the future. Suffering is part of the divine plan and is essential to our exaltation. This life is "a preparatory state given to finite beings, a space wherein they may improve themselves for a higher state of being." (*Discourses of Brigham Young*, p. 345.) Those unwilling to withstand adversity will not be exalted. "Hatred and persecutions have been the lot of every man that ever lived on the earth holding the oracles of the Kingdom of Heaven to deliver to the children of men." (Brigham Young, JD 7:198.) We must pass through the refining experience of sorrow as did Enoch, Noah, Melchizedek, Abraham, Isaac, and Jacob if we are to enjoy with them the blessings of the celestial kingdom.

As the New Testament emphasizes, we are in a sorry state if it is only in this life that we have hope in Christ. (See 1 Corinthians 15:19.) Having that hope, that faith in Christ, we have anticipation of a Lazareth-like deliverance from the pains of our present estate. We are told that man is that he might have joy. (See 2 Nephi 2:25.) And yet even Eve knew that we must suffer to really experience joy. (See Moses 5:11.)

What is the purpose of suffering? It has its place in the divine plan. When we are moved to cry out to the Lord, "Let this cup pass me by," let us remember, "Thy will be done, not mine." When we lose a loved one, let us be concerned with the deepening of life rather than its lengthening.

Against the Mystery
of Death

Richard L. Evans

We come again to the most urgent questions of life: What is man? Where did he come from? Why is he here? Where does he go? What is the meaning, the purpose, of life? What is the assurance of everlasting life? In searching deeply for the answers, we would cite some lines of certainty and assurance on the reality of the resurrection: "Against the . . . mystery of . . . death—comes this glory of the risen Christ, this victory of the spirit over the weakness of the body, this disclosure of immortality, not as a vision but as a fact. . . . Hosts of men and women would live their lives in all purity and honor [even] if they knew there was no fair country beyond the gates of death; many men and women *are* living in heroic constancy and patience without that [assurance]. . . . But if that hope were to die out of society, the light would go out of the world, . . . the mystery of life would degenerate into a meaningless tragedy. The . . . rising of one man out of the grave, the triumph of one spirit over death has changed all life, and made the world a home instead of a sepulcher. . . ." (*The Outlook*, April 22, 1905.) Our eternal continuance is assured, but "the modern world is full of unhappiness because it is full of unbelief. . . . To be happy in such an age as this is the first duty of every man who believes in God and his care for his children; for happiness is the state of those who know that, while all kinds of pain and sorrow may meet them on the way . . .

"The Spoken Word" from Temple Square, presented over KSL and the Columbia Broadcasting System, March 29, 1964. Copyright 1964. Reprinted in *Improvement Era*, June 1966, p. 524.

there is nevertheless a divine purpose being worked out. . . . Men need the joy and freedom of a great renewal of faith; . . . let them take counsel with their noblest aspirations instead of with the . . . despair of those . . . who rest [life's] mysteries without the light of the Resurrection; let them rest not in the guidance of their fellows, blind and baffled like themselves . . ." (*The Outlook*, April 22, 1906) but in Him who showed the way and who gave us the assurance that life is purposeful and everlasting. Thank God for the reality of the resurrection, and for the awareness that loved ones await us in literal personal reality beyond the limits of this life. "I know that my redeemer liveth." (Job 19:25.)

Distinctions in the Mormon Approach to Death and Dying

Truman G. Madsen

This symposium* corroborates a recent essay on "Dying with Dignity" that reports a "crescendo of concern" about dying and death.[1] The concern shows up in books, journals, conferences, television programs, societies. Yet, at the same time, it is observed that, whereas the facts of life were hidden from youth in a former generation, the facts of death seem to be a conversational taboo today. How does one reconcile this deliberate avalanche of discussion and studied silence?

A score of writers would argue that this paradox arises because we try to make death a "thing" outside of us—vague, anonymous, removed—an escape from the gnawing awareness in all of us that we must die. Our preoccupation can be deliberately ignored as it is in silence, or it can emerge in all kinds of brave verbal objectifications.

If Latter-day Saints are unimpressed by these trends, it is not due, I suspect, to isolation or insulation from the real world. It is because there are root assurances that go deep and overbeliefs that go high; these preside over and temper all of our attitudes. In this paper I wish to address ten such roots of Mormon assurance that are powerful in their patterning effect.

My title uses the word "distinctions." The first question

---

*Symposium sponsored by the Religious Studies Center April 13-14, 1977. Talks published in Spencer J. Palmer, ed., *Deity and Death* (Religious Studies Center, Brigham Young University, 1978), pp. 61-76.

is, are the distinctions distinctive? In three ways they are not: First, if one looks deeply into historic religions, he can find precedent, parallel, and in some cases identity in the teachings of this dispensation and those of former ones. Second, the response to death, both in individuals and in institutions, undergoes change. Our great-grandfathers may have had significantly different attitudes about death, though they belonged to the same or a most similar religious movement. Third, the doctrinal or teaching core of the Church on this theme is overlaid with multiple ever-expanding cultures. Many of the variable customs and traditions of other cultures may or may not be harmonious with this gospel outlook but continue to have residual influence on the convert.

Plurality

One striking insight in the Mormon scriptures on death is that there are many kinds. The word itself is often used in the plural, "deaths," in exact juxtaposition to the word "lives." The point here is not simply that there are many ways of reaching the final event of mortality, it is, rather, that while we are more or less alive here, there are many possible dyings. Without being too precise, one finds in the scriptures at least four characterizations of death: (1) Death is absence from the presence of God. (2) Death is the wages of sin—the loss of life intensity. It is, for example, darkness of mind, hardness of heart and numbness of conscience. These are the deaths in the self which may precede death of the body. The deceased is diseased spiritually. (3) Death is the separation of the spirit from the body. (4) Death is the discontinuation of life powers. This is the opposite of what section 132 calls "the fullness and continuation of the seeds"—a delimitation on creative and pro-creative power.

The role of Christ is to overcome all of these deaths in us, both as prevention and redemption. To gain victory over every form of death is the essence of life. Preoccupation with the third kind, the event, is a sign of confusion: soul-sickness. "Salvation consists in overcoming all one's enemies. The last enemy is death."

Death and God

In the world's major religions, the question of God and the question of immortality are often separate: one may affirm the one and deny the other. Belief in immortality has never been strong among the Jews, for example, yet belief in God has been vigorous. Among philosophers, Charles Hartshorne is not alone in affirming a life-giving and fully perfected God who not only permits but requires that man disappear forever. On the other hand, there are those who affirm immortality and deny God. Scientists today, by no means mad scientists, seriously reach for the dream of Ponce de Leon. Some say we will be capable of immortality before the turn of the century. We may even opt to die with tentative rights for a rerun on the demand of our survivors—blanking out for periods and blinking in for other periods. Then the folk witticism would be practical: "If the rich could hire others to die, a poor man could make a living." (Sholem Aleichem.)

Mormonism, whatever the triumphs of the scientists, equates God, immortality, and resurrection. Life in its highest mode requires all three. There is a difference between surviving forever and living forever. One who achieves eternal life must have become like the eternal who has mastered life—he must be perfect.

What Death Does to Life

In contemporary discussion, opposite attitudes arise as one faces imminent death. For Martin Heidegger, man at his best is committed to whatever he does as *Sein-zum-Tode*—being unto death. For him, the consciousness of death at this level is intertwined with the sense of the passing of time, projects, and guilt. On different grounds, Jean-Paul Sartre and Camus affirm the essence of "living on the underground," the constant threat of death as somehow leading to the existential virtue of authenticity. One is most alive when he is closest to death. On other grounds, Viktor Frankl recalls his prison camp experience as his clearest and closest understanding of love.

For Joseph Smith, death is indeed the outside limit and

sometimes the cost of a Christ-like mission. There may be slow martyrdom, as when one "wastes and wears out his life" in bringing to light hidden things of darkness. "Be faithful, even if you should be slain," he was told early. Or death may fulfill, atone, redeem. "Do not be alarmed, brethren, for they can only do what they did to the ancient saints. They can only kill the body." To the degree that this statement of Joseph Smith in the menace of a mob comforted his brethren, they had caught the vision. But notice that for Joseph Smith death was not a mere incident because the body is cheap or worthless. Rather, it was because the body is finally indestructible. The quality of man's resurrection depends upon his response to the way of Christ. To preserve the mortal body by betrayal of Christ is a death worse than death.

The Body As Enemy

In many religions, ancient and modern, the body is viewed as an impediment to the spiritual life, a prison or as Plato put it, "an outlandish slough," a Gnostic prison. Among Buddhists the body or *skhanda* is finally recognized as inferior and even as unreal. So likewise in Christian Science. In the religions of escape in the Far East, persistence of life in the body is viewed as the extension of *karma*, a kind of punishment. And where the objective is not utter annihilation, the body is to be deprived and mortified but with the high aim to achieve the extinction of desire. In monastic Catholic traditions and pious Protestant ones, there is a similar effort, often ascribed to Paul, that takes initiative in asceticism. Gandhi expressed two world traditions, occidental and oriental, in saying he wished he had never experienced fleshly impulses.

Contrary to these views, much Greek philosophical theology, and the flesh-disparagements of Augustine and Calvin, Mormonism teaches:

1. That "we came into the world to receive a body and present it pure before God in the Celestial Kingdom." That oppression in our pre-embodied condition arose because we lacked a body.

"All beings who have bodies have power over those who have not."[2]

As Joseph Smith put it, "The express purpose of God in giving it (the spirit) a tabernacle was to arm it against the power of darkness."[3] And elsewhere he taught that unembodied intelligences did not have power to defend themselves against those that had a tabernacle. It is a privilege to be in the body, even a crippled, handicapped, diseased body.

2. That the purpose of life is not to transcend the flesh but to transform it. "The great principle of happiness consists in having a body."

3. That a fulness of joy is impossible without the inseparable connection of spirit and body. "When separated man cannot receive a fulness of joy." (D&C 93:33.)

4. That we should improve the time of this mortal probation because, "A man can do as much in this life in one year as he can do in ten years in the spirit world without the body."[4]

5. That the strong will to endure life, even in the midst of pain, has been divinely planted in us in order that we might cling to life and thus accomplish the designs of our Creator. So said Joseph Smith to Wilford Woodruff.[5]

6. That there is some truth in the comment, "The good die young," because, as Joseph speculated, they are "too pure, too lovely to live upon the earth."[6] Yet in the long view Joseph Smith taught, "I do not like to see a little child pass away, for it has not filled the measure of its creation and gained the victory over death."[7] Children, of course, are innocent, but they are not experienced. They will yet have opportunities of reckoning in the flesh with experience and contrast, if only in the post-millennial struggle. They are assured salvation in the celestial kingdom, but only when they have fulfilled the conditions will they enjoy the highest exaltation.

7. That desire, fulfillment of desires and increased refinement of desire, are eternal processes.

8. That death as a separation process is an enemy. The spirit may properly crave death (due to the decline of age, disease, and the imprisoning effects of sin), but we will look

upon the absence of our spirits from our bodies as "a bondage." (D&C 45:17.)

Selective vs. Universal Immortality

Many world religions hold that death is universal but that immortality is extremely selective, reserved for the elite, the few, the 144,000, the fit, the enlightened ones, or whatever. (Some religions deny that some men even have souls and have certainly excluded animals and the lower forms of life.) Joseph Smith said, "All are born to die. And all men must rise." "All must enter eternity." Man is not an endangered species.

As for other forms of life, Joseph Smith taught, "Every living thing that knows enough to run when you point your finger at it will be resurrected."[8] That means not just beasts, fish, and birds; it means ants, beetles (of whom there are nine thousand known species), and mosquitoes. Joseph taught that John's apocalypse speaks of beasts in heaven, not only in rich symbolisms, but in literal description: there are beasts in heaven. He taught, according to Benjamin F. Johnson, that all the animal kingdoms resurrected "would remain in the dominion and therefore the stewardship of those who, with creative power, reach out for dominion through the power of endless lives." He expected, he said, to meet his black horse Joe Duncan and his faithful dog Major.

The Earth Glorified

If life is precious in animal form, it is also precious in plant and mineral. God commends all life. The earth itself is organic, somehow alive. In the sense of separation of spirit and body, it will eventually die. It will die, moreover, innocently. Unlike rebellious man, the earth flawlessly fills the measure of its creation—obeys the law of its organizer. Too often man has not replenished but exploited, not sanctified but polluted, not redeemed but corrupted the earth. The earth has been baptized by immersion, it will likewise be baptized in the Spirit by fire, be renewed to its paradisiacal state, and glorified to a beauty beyond descrip-

tion. (See D&C 84:25-26.) It will then return to its position
in the cosmos from which it was removed after the fall of
man. It will be "rolled back into the presence of God." Not
the least but the most righteous will inherit it.

Thus the history of Mother Earth recapitulates the history of sanctified mankind. And it is a type, a foreshadow-
ing, of more and more worlds that are more and more alive,
abundant, and abounding. Christ and the resurrected Saints
will reign upon it during the one thousand years, but not
permanently, for they will thereafter "come and go, visiting and governing the earth." So Edward L. Stevenson
heard Joseph say.[9] The kinship of life and life will be complete. There will be no need for C. S. Lewis's imaginative
proposal for rewarding insects. "A heaven for mosquitoes
could be combined with a hell for man." Heaven will be
the same for both.

Is All of Real Man Immortal?

It is not uncommon in world religions to hold that only
one aspect or fragment of faculty or mode of man will live
on. For Plato, this is the immaterial soul. For Aristotle, it is
nous or reason. For the Buddhists, it is the ultimate nature
of the enlightened *bodhi* in a distinctionless nirvana. For
the Christian Scientist, it is pure mind.

Joseph Smith taught that all of real man is immortal:
mind, spirit and body. Therefore the analogy of similarity
between the conditions we know here and the conditions
hereafter is thorough-going. But there are crucial differences. The most vital change between the present corruptible body and the incorrupt resurrection is that the glorified
body will have within it not blood, but a spirit fluid. "Flesh
and blood cannot go there, but flesh and bones quickened
by the Spirit of God can."[10] For Joseph Smith, there are
everlasting spirals of unfolding involvement, self-sacrificing
love—"all heights and all depths." Eternal lives will include the contemplative, the active, and the creative
modes, greatly intensified into the magnificence of celestial
joy.

The notion of transmigration of souls or of successive

mortal rebirths or of switching species was labeled by Joseph Smith as "a doctrine of the devil."[11]

The doctrine is wrongheaded for three reasons: First, "All men must die and all must rise" (in their own bodies). This is the law. It cancels out all variations of doctrines of body switching or soul sleeping, as also of annihilation. Second, there is no crossover of kinds. Men do not become cockroaches, nor vice versa; sacred cows do not become gods. Our body, the body we have now in its essential elements is ours forever. The decision to accept embodiment was voluntary. Now that it is made, it is irreversible. Your body is as permanently yours as you are permanently you. Even the sons of perdition will be resurrected.

Third, there is only one mortal probation, and it is crucial. There are stages before and stages after, and one may indeed move in the cyclic spiral, but not in repetition and not in a circle. The seriousness, the risk, and the glories of mortal life are undercut the moment one supposes he will have a million or more subsequent probations of the same sort. It is a spurious comfort to be told, as was the weeping wife at the cremation of her husband in India, "Do not weep, he has been through this a million times before." Physically and metaphysically that is impossible.

This also means that ontological suicide—the craving for annihilation—is a will-o'-the wisp. The positive gospel message is: we must learn to live with ourselves.

The Quantity-Quality Controversy

Many who believe immortality is an illusion, religious humanists for example, insist that both suicide and euthanasia are a human right. If there is, as Freud taught, a death wish, some claim that it is more than a desire to end this predicament and indeed all predicaments; it is a desire for "the catastrophe which ends all catastrophe." Will Durant says, in effect, that after writing thirty-five volumes, "eternal sleep will be welcome." Other humanists argue that there is something hypocritical, spurious, or projective about the religious notion that one should live for the next life instead of for this one. Secular critics such as Marx and

Feurbrach plead for living exclusively in the here and now.

No religion has been as effective as Mormonism in uniting the traditional split between the here and now and the then and there. The spirit and body are inseparably connected; so in the temples are heaven and earth; so are joy and sorrow; so are life and death. When Henry P. Van Dusen, president of Union Theological Seminary, and his wife committed suicide, some defended their right. But others, feeling this was a betrayal of both life and death, said sadly, "We do not read in the New Testament that man has a right, on his own, to decide when to lay down his cross." Mormons share that conviction.

The Family As an Individual

Much of Judeo-Christian theology doubts or denies individual immortality: so do scientific materialists. The self is swallowed up in some cosmic reservoir, as absolute as in Bertrand Russell's "vast, total death of the solar system." Some have nevertheless offered the comfort of "social immortality." This means that one is replicated in his posterity, or at least in the memory of friends.

We have observed that Joseph Smith teaches individual identity in perpetuity in both directions. In this sense, our individual immortality is in no way contingent on that of others. On the other hand, the highest immortality is a family affair. In that sense we are either exalted together or not at all. Thus, others are crucial to the quality and intensity of our own eternal lives. Husband and wife become "one" in their children. But parents are themselves linked to an unbroken chain of forebears. This is a clarification of the great Israelite insight that all Israel and ultimately all mankind stand accountable and privileged before God as one individual. We do not overcome what Joseph Smith called the "last enemy," which is death, until we perceive that "they without us and we without them cannot be made perfect," hence the indispensability of sealing in its highest, deepest sense. This is the core of truth in the oriental notion that our ancestors may both plague us and bless us. The positive truth is that to some extent they may redeem us as we them, and that our highest transformation is intertwined with theirs.

We may miss this crucial point when we say that the resurrection is unconditional, but that redemption from sin is conditional upon Christ. In fact, the thatness of *a* resurrection is inevitable. But the when, the how, the where, and the by whom; the withness of our and their resurrection, is contingent not only on Brother Christ but on all brothers elder and younger, the whole family of Christ. In no world religion is this theme more central, more conscious, and more extensively carried out in action.

Death and Fatalism

Is the time of death preset? There are determinist religions that say yes. Among the Greek Stoics, submission to the necessity of death, including its timing, was the essence of wisdom. Among the Romans, the Greek idea of *moira* or destiny became the trump card of human courage. Shakespeare has Julius Caesar say he has no fear because "Death, a necessary end, will come when it will come." In the Orient there is *Kismet* (fate), a denial at times of any chance or voluntary factors in the life and death process. In America we are told that one of every five citizens today believes somehow in astrology, and among the things the stars are believed to control is the time of death. The man who asked the spiritualist where he was going to die exclaimed, "I'll never go there!" But the point of Greek tragedy, as of modern determinism, is that we have no choice.

Mormonism is not with the fatalists. It is true that modern revelation speaks of being "appointed unto death." (D&C 42:48.) And the Prophet Joseph Smith was promised in Liberty Jail, "Thy days are known, and thy years shall not be numbered less." (D&C 122:9.) (The inference is also, shall not be numbered more.) The assurance is not uncommon among Latter-day Saints that whereas the wicked may shorten their lives, the righteous are taken only when "their time" has come.

In fact, these promises are all conditional. Life may be

prolonged by the united efforts of the faithful. Joseph's exact promise was that *if* he hearkened unto the voice of the Spirit, he had *about* five years to live. The "if" clause, as well as the inexactness of the time, left room for his initiative. Promises to the faithful of protection, of fulfillment of missions, of safety arise not as an independent, relentless, grinding fate, but as the result of a free-willed covenant relationship in which both the will of man and the will of God collide. Only so long as one is true and faithful does one have promise; otherwise he has none.

Mourning Customs

The variations on meeting the dazing shock of death are almost infinite. Among the Jews, the first response is a *shiva*, a seven-day period of mourning. One remains at home, seated in the midst of sympathizing friends. Then comes *shloshim;* one avoids places of entertainment and follows ritual prayers. For parents this is followed by a full year of mourning. Comparable practices exist in other world religions.

Among the Mormons there is no valorizing or ceremonializing of mourning, though there is a characteristic funeral. Modern revelation admonishes, "Thou shalt weep for the loss of thy loved ones, especially those who have not hope of a glorious resurrection." The promise "Those that die in me shall not taste [the bitterness of] death, for it shall be sweet unto them" (D&C 42:46) extends often to those bereaved. When death comes at a ripe climax of a life well lived, there is a noticeable absence of agony, a fervent sense of culmination, and even, at times, rejoicing.

Having worked four years in a cemetery, witnessing funerals, graveside rituals, and patterns of almost every nationality, tradition, and emotional tone, I can report this: the closest analogy to a Mormon funeral at graveside is a missionary farewell. Here is a group of loved ones, not hard-faced and stoical, not blank and numb, but sensitized. There is apparent grief, but not despair. There is warmth and promise. This may be caught up in the words of Wilford Woodruff and then in a list of impressions otherwise unaccountable. First, President Woodruff:

". . . I wish my body washed clean and clothed in clean white linen, according to the order of the Holy Priesthood, and put into a plain, decent coffin, made of native wood, with plenty of room. *I do not wish any black made use of about my coffin, or about the vehicle that conveys my body to the grave.* I do not wish my family or friends *to wear any badge of mourning for me* at my funeral or afterwards, for, if I am true and faithful unto death, there will be no necessity for anyone to mourn for me. . . . Their speech will be to the living. *If the laws and customs of the spirit world will permit, I should wish to attend my funeral but I shall be governed by the counsel I receive in the spirit world.*" [12]

Now the list of impressions:

— The ancient mother who cheerfully sews her own white burial clothes.
— The widely known speaker who tapes his own funeral sermon and sparkles it with his verve for life.
— A gathering, as death hovers close, to appoint a celestial mailman. Messages to be delivered to loved ones on the other side. "Give my love to Mother," or "Tell Aunt Martha we're doing fine." Here is absent the curious etiquette that forbids that even a husband and wife use the word "death" when one knows clearly that one is on his deathbed.
— Humor that is neither grizzly nor forced, that enables a man emerging from a stroke to wink his one good eye and say to the family anxiously surrounding his bed, "I fooled you!"
— Addressing the deceased at the funeral or graveside as if she or he is present.
— The smile that so often attends the faithful, as if the last mortal facial set was in recognition of a beckoning loved one.
— The sense of mission in the military. Facing death is the price of Christ's way.
— The music which resembles a hymnal rhapsody rather than the darkening dirge. "And may there be no sadness of farewell, when I embark." (Tennyson.)
— The jibe of a J. Golden Kimball: "I can't wait to die to see if all this stuff we've been teaching is true,"

combined with the sober testimony, "When I meet my
Father, I know he will understand me, and that is more
than you have been able to do."
— Prompt and some would say sudden remarriage. Joseph
Smith followed the early custom of thinking marriage
within three months was unkind to the memory of the
dead but reversed himself when he counseled his
brother Hyrum to marry "without delay."[13]

Sacred Ground

Is the burial place sacred? In many religions, yes.
Trespass onto Indian burial grounds is met with capital
punishment. The excessive luxuriance of the pharaohs in
mummification, rich artifacts, and pyramidal protection is
an attempt to foil the sacrilege of gravediggers. In many
churches, Catholic and Protestant, over the centuries the
right to be buried in or near the churchyard has functioned
as a spiritual badge or as posthumous excommunication.

Mormonism both affirms and denies these traditions. On
the one hand, Joseph Smith praised and reembodied the
desires of the ancient Joseph to have his bones brought back
to the family tomb in Shechem. Before he undertook the
perilous Zion's Camp march, he charged Brigham Young to
bring his body back to Kirtland. "I command you to do it in
the name of Israel's God," and learning that missionary Lorenzo Barnes was being buried on foreign soil, he developed
that theme. Late in 1844 he told his trusted brethren Al-
pheus Cutler and Reynolds Cahoon that he wanted to be
buried by his father in a Nauvoo tomb, unless his enemies
preempted his body as they had threatened. Likewise, he
made the same request of Emma. John Taylor recalls his
reason for this; it was future-oriented:

"I heard Joseph Smith say at the time he was making a
tomb at Nauvoo that he expected when the time came,
when the grave would be rent asunder, that he would arise
and embrace his father and mother, and shake hands with
his friends. It was his written request that when he died,
some kind friends would see he was buried near his bosom
friends, so that when he and they arose in the morning of

the First Resurrection, he could embrace them, saying, 'My father! My mother!' "[14]

One reading of much that I have said is that, for the Mormons, death is an illusion. There could not be a more fatal mistake. The mortal predicament is not simply that we have a deadline beyond which the body will temporarily dissolve; it is that while still in the body, we may so imbibe the poisons of sin that we suffer, in more or less degree, the permanent blows of death. One key for understanding all of the ordinances of the gospel, beginning with the rebirths of baptism and culminating in the sealings of the temple, is that all are instruments of overcoming both death *of* the body and death *in* the body.

In Mormon theology the adversary is the arch-destroyer; his diabolical objective is to clip the wings of life. To the degree that he diminishes life he is winning, as we are losing. It is a tragic confusion to suppose that his winning is temporary. He has already won one-third of the hosts of heaven against embodiment, plunging them into a lasting death. He is in a life-and-death struggle with all of mankind on an even broader scale. We may rejoice that "all will be saved except the sons of perdition." But to be saved, even to be exalted in a delimited condition is to be partially damned.

Jacob prays: "May God raise you from death by the power of the resurrection, and also from everlasting death by the power of the atonement, that ye may be received into the eternal kingdom of God, that ye may praise him through grace divine. Amen." (2 Nephi 10:25.)

NOTES

1. Foreword to "The Favor of the Gods," annual oration of the Society for Health and Human Values, by Ronald Berman, San Francisco, California, November 11, 1976.

2. From William Clayton's book, p. 8, MS 188, Brigham Young University Special Collections, Provo, Utah.

3. See Minute Book of William P. McIntyre, January 8, 1840-April 20, 1845, MSC 1014, Historical Department of The Church of Jesus Christ of Latter-day Saints, Salt Lake City, Utah.

4. See Oliver B. Huntington in *They Knew the Prophet* (Salt Lake City: Bookcraft, 1974), p. 61.

5. See Diary of Charles L. Walker, August 1877, St. George, Utah, p. 576, BYU Special Collections.

6. Joseph Smith, *Teachings of the Prophet Joseph Smith*, comp. Joseph Fielding Smith (Salt Lake City: Deseret Book Co., 1938), p. 196.

7. See *Early History of Provo*, 1849-1872; Utah Stake Bishop Meetings, July 17, 1868.

8. Young Woman's Journal 5:490.
9. Edward L. Stevenson, *Life of Edward Stevenson*, BYU Special Collections, p. 104.
10. *Teachings of the Prophet Joseph Smith*, p. 326.
11. *Teachings of the Prophet Joseph Smith*, pp. 104-5.
12. Matthias Cowley, "Wilford Woodruff," Deseret News, 1909, p. 622.
13. *Teachings of the Prophet Joseph Smith*, p. 120.
14. John Taylor, *Gospel Kingdom* (Salt Lake City: Bookcraft, 1943), p. 23.

Confronting Our Own Death

The Dead Who Die in the Lord

Bruce R. McConkie

I shall speak of a subject that strikes dread—even terror—into the hearts of most men. It is something we fear, of which we are sorely afraid, and from which most of us would flee if we could.

I shall speak of the passing of the immortal soul into the eternal realms ahead, of that dread day when we shall shuffle off this mortal coil and go back to the dust from whence we came. I shall speak of death—mortal death, the natural death, the death of the body—and of the state of the souls of men when this final consummation is imposed upon them.

Manifestly, we must all be guided and enlightened by the power of the Holy Spirit as we step into this realm, this realm of which carnal men know so little, but of which so much has been revealed to the saints of the Most High.

I pray that my words, spoken by the power of the Holy Ghost, shall sink deeply into your hearts by the power of that same Spirit, so that you will know of their truth and verity.

For a text I take these sweet and consoling words of biblical origin: "Precious in the sight of the Lord is the death of his saints." (Psalm 116:15.) To them I append Paul's pointed and painful pronouncement: "The sting of death is sin." (1 Corinthians 15:56.)

Death can be comforting and sweet and precious or it can thrust upon us all the agonies and sulphurous burnings

Address delivered at the 146th Semiannual General Conference of the Church, October 1976. Published in *Ensign*, November 1976, pp. 106-8.

of an endless hell. And we—each of us individually—make the choice as to which it shall be.

If we are to place death in its proper perspective in the eternal scheme of things, we must first learn the purposes of life. We must know whence we came, Whose we are, and why He placed us here. Only then can we envision whither we shall yet go in the providences of Him who made us.

We know, because the Lord has revealed it in this our day, that we are the spirit children of an exalted, glorified Being, a Holy Man who has a body of flesh and bones and who is our Father in heaven.

We know that the name of the kind of life He lives is *eternal life* and that it consists of living in the family unit and of possessing all power, all might, and all dominion.

We know that He ordained and established the plan of salvation to enable us to advance and progress from our spirit state, to the same state of glory, honor, and exaltation which He Himself possesses.

We know that the Father's plan called for the creation of this earth, where we could dwell as mortals, receive bodies made of the dust of the earth, and undergo the tests and trials which now face us.

We know that this plan of salvation included provisions for the fall of man, with its consequent temporal and spiritual death; for a redemption from death through the atoning sacrifice of the Son of God; and for an inheritance of eternal life for all the obedient.

We know that this great plan of progression called for a *birth* which would provide a mortal tabernacle for our eternal spirits, and for a *death* which would free those spirits from the frailties, diseases, and weaknesses of mortality.

And may I say that this life never was intended to be easy. It is a probationary estate in which we are tested physically, mentally, morally, and spiritually. We are subject to disease and decay. We are attacked by cancer, leprosy, and contagious diseases. We suffer pain and sorrow and afflictions. Disasters strike; floods sweep away our homes; famines destroy our food; plagues and wars fill our graves with dead bodies and our broken homes with sorrow.

We are called upon to choose between the revealed word of God and the soul-destroying postulates of the theoretical sciences. Temptations, the lusts of the flesh, evils of every sort—all these are part of the plan, and must be faced by every person privileged to undergo the experiences of mortality.

The testing processes of mortality are for all men, saints and sinners alike. Sometimes the tests and trials of those who have received the gospel far exceed any imposed upon worldly people. Abraham was called upon to sacrifice his only son. Lehi and his family left their lands and wealth to live in a wilderness. Saints in all ages have been commanded to lay all that they have upon the altar, sometimes even their very lives.

As to the individual trials and problems that befall any of us, all we need say is that in the wisdom of Him who knows all things, and who does all things well, all of us are given the particular and specific tests that we need in our personal situations. It is to us, His saints, that the Lord speaks when He says: "I will prove you in all things, whether you will abide in my covenant, even unto death, that you may be found worthy.

"For if ye will not abide in my covenant ye are not worthy of me." (D&C 98:14-15.)

Now, what of death? of the passing of loved ones? of our life beyond the grave?

Our scriptures say: "Death hath passed upon all men, to fulfil the merciful plan of the great Creator." (2 Nephi 9:6.) Where the true Saints are concerned there is no sorrow in death except that which attends a temporary separation from loved ones. Birth and death are both essential steps in the unfolding drama of eternity.

We shouted for joy at the privilege of becoming mortal because without the tests of mortality there could be no eternal life. We now sing praises to the great Redeemer for the privilege of passing from this life because without death and the resurrection we could not be raised in immortal glory and gain eternal life.

When the faithful saints depart from this life they "are received into a state of happiness, which is called paradise, a state of rest, a state of peace, where they shall rest from all their troubles and from all care, and sorrow" (Alma 40:12), and they remain in this state until the day of their resurrection.

When the wicked and ungodly depart from this life they continue in their wickedness and rebellion. "That same spirit which doth possess your bodies at the time ye go out of this life," the scripture says, "that same spirit will have power to possess your body in that eternal world." (Alma 34:34.)

"Ye must press forward with a steadfastness in Christ," Nephi said to members of the Church, "having a perfect brightness of hope, and a love of God and of all men. Wherefore, if ye shall press forward, feasting upon the word of Christ, and endure to the end, behold, thus saith the Father: Ye shall have eternal life." (2 Nephi 31:20.) That is to say—all the faithful Saints, all of those who have endured to the end, depart this life with the absolute guarantee of eternal life.

There is no equivocation, no doubt, no uncertainty in our minds. Those who have been true and faithful in this life will not fall by the wayside in the life to come. If they keep their covenants here and now and depart this life firm and true in the testimony of our blessed Lord, they shall come forth with an inheritance of eternal life.

We do not mean to say that those who die in the Lord, and who are true and faithful in this life, must be perfect in all things when they go into the next sphere of existence. There was only one perfect man—the Lord Jesus whose Father was God.

There have been many righteous souls who have attained relative degrees of perfection, and there have been great hosts of faithful people who have kept the faith, and lived the law, and departed this life with the full assurance of an eventual inheritance of eternal life.

There are many things they will do and must do, even beyond the grave, to merit the fulness of the Father's kingdom in that final glorious day when the great King shall say unto them, "Come, ye blessed of my Father, inherit the kingdom prepared for you from the foundation of the world." (Matthew 25:34.)

But what we are saying is that when the saints of God chart a course of righteousness, when they gain sure testimonies of the truth and divinity of the Lord's work, when they keep the commandments, when they overcome the world, when they put first in their lives the things of God's kingdom: when they do all these things, and then depart this life—though they have not yet become perfect—they shall nonetheless gain eternal life in our Father's kingdom; and eventually they shall be perfect as God their Father and Christ His Son are perfect.

Is it any wonder that the scriptures say: "Precious in the sight of the Lord is the death of his saints"? (Psalm 116:15.) Truly such is precious, wondrous, and glorious, for when the saints die, added souls have assured themselves of exaltation with Him who provided the way for them to advance and progress and become like Him.

Is it any wonder that the scriptures say: "Blessed are the dead which die in the Lord," for they shall "rest from their labours; and their works do follow them." (Revelation 14:13.) Truly it is a blessed occasion, for the faithful saints have filled the full measure of their creation, and a gracious God will give them all things in due course.

Is it any wonder that the Lord says to His saints, "Those that die in me shall not taste of death, for it shall be sweet unto them"? (D&C 42:46.)

Is it any wonder that the Prophet Joseph Smith said such things as: "When men are prepared, they are better off to go hence"? (*Teachings of the Prophet Joseph Smith*, p. 326.)

"Those who have died in Jesus Christ may expect to enter into all that fruition of joy when they come forth, which they possessed or anticipated here." (*Teachings*, p. 295.)

"In the resurrection, some are raised to be angels, others are raised to become Gods." (*Teachings*, p. 312.)

Now, we do not seek death, though it is part of the merciful plan of the great Creator. Rather we rejoice in life, and desire to live as long as we can be of service to our fellowmen. Faithful saints are a leaven of righteousness in a wicked world.

But sometimes the Lord's people are hounded and persecuted. Sometimes He deliberately lets His faithful saints linger and suffer, in both body and spirit, to prove them in all things, and to see if they will abide in His covenant, even unto death, that they may be found worthy of eternal life. If such be the lot of any of us, so be it.

But come what may, anything that befalls us here in mortality is but for a small moment, and if we are true and faithful God will eventually exalt us on high. All our losses and sufferings will be made up to us in the resurrection.

We shall be raised from mortality to immortality, from corruption to incorruption. We shall come forth from the grave in physical perfection. Not a hair of the head shall be lost, and God shall wipe away all tears.

If we have lived the gospel we shall come forth with celestial bodies which are prepared to stand the glory of a celestial kingdom. We shall continue to live in the family unit, and as Joseph Smith said, "That same sociality which exists among us here will exist among us there, only it will be coupled with eternal glory, which glory we do not now enjoy." (D&C 130:2.)

We rejoice in life. We rejoice in death. We have no desires except to do the will of Him whose we are and to dwell with Him in His kingdom at the appointed time.

O that it might be with each of us as it was with that valiant apostle of old who said, as the hour of his death approached:

"I am now ready to be offered, and the time of my departure is at hand.

"I have fought a good fight, I have finished my course, I have kept the faith:

"Henceforth there is laid up for me a crown of righteousness, which the Lord, the righteous judge, shall give me at that day: and not to me only, but unto all them also that love his appearing." (2 Timothy 4:6-8.)

In the name of the Lord Jesus Christ. Amen.

Fear Not Death

Hugh B. Brown

I am persuaded that the reason many men are afraid of
death is because they are afraid of the unknown. They say,
and rightly, that we know really very little about the pattern and detail of what is over there. The Lord hasn't
revealed very much about the details of that life, but that
there is such a life He has made plain through repeated
revelation. . . . One reason that some men are afraid of
death is that they say that no one has come back to tell
what happens there. They say, "I am afraid to go because
while I know what is happening here, I don't know what is
going to be [there]." When I hear a man speak like that, I
think and sometimes ask him, "How much did you know
about this world before you came into it? Were you afraid
to come?"

According to the scriptures, we shouted for joy at the
prospects, although I am sure we knew something of the
risk involved. We were not afraid in one sense, for we had
some knowledge. However, when we entered that prenatal
state where our bodies were being formed, we began to
forget what we had learned in a pre-existent state, and in
that state just before our mortal birth, if someone could
have talked with us as unborn babes, and had said to us individually, "You are to be born into another world shortly,"
I am quite sure if the little child could speak or think, he
would have shrunk back and said, "I don't want to be born
into another world. I am happy here under the heart of my

From an address at the funeral of Christen Jensen, August 21, 1961. Printed in *Instructor*,
December 1961, pp. 404-5.

mother. Separate me from her, and I must die. Don't ask me to be born into an unknown world. I fear it." I think perhaps that is what a child would say. The remarkable thing is that when the child is born—and if it had not been born in due course, it would have died, and the mother, too, perhaps—he finds an environment suited to him. He finds that during the months of preparation he has been developing certain functional organs which were not needed in that prenatal state, but which immediately began to operate when the child breathed the first breath of life; the lungs and other organs of the body began to function.

Now I wonder, brethren and sisters, whether in a very real sense this earth life is not a prenatal state. Prenatal meaning before birth. I personally am very sure that that is true. This is a preparatory state. If that is true, then we are now, perhaps, largely, unconsciously, developing certain, shall we call them spiritual organs, which we do not fully utilize, but which when we are born into that next life will begin to operate and function. We shall find there as we have found here that preparation was made for our coming, not only in the environment, but in ourselves.

What we call death is but a birth and a beginning, and we need not fear this change.

To Die Well

Sterling W. Sill

Two of the most important events in life are birth and death. And what a thrilling thing it is to be well born, to have goodly parents and live in a godly home! But it may be even more important to die well. Sometime ago in this general conference, I talked about the importance of birth and the life that follows it. This morning I would like to say something about the importance of death and the life that follows it.

Sometimes we miss one of our best opportunities—to learn to die well—because we think of death as unpleasant. And because we don't like to think about unpleasant things, we sometimes close our minds and turn away our faces. But death doesn't cease to exist just because it is ignored. The ancient Egyptians had a much more logical way of handling this situation when on their great festive occasions they kept constantly on display before the revelers the skeleton of a dead man. That is, they held up this great image of death before themselves that each one might be continually and constantly reminded that some day he would die.

Now I don't want to frighten anyone unduly in this audience this morning, but I would like to point out as gently and as kindly as I can that someday this tremendously important experience of our mortal estate will come to its end. Someone has said that judging by the past there will be very few of us who get out of this world

Address delivered at the 146th Semiannual General Conference of the Church. Published in *Ensign*, November 1976, pp. 46-48.

alive. From the very beginning of life, each one of us lives under an irrevocable, unchangeable death sentence, with a guarantee that it will be carried out. The Lord has given us this maximum notice to enable us to adequately prepare for it. And one man indicated this certainty by an inscription on his tombstone saying, "I knew it would happen!"

The other night I reread the old Grecian tragedy written around the fall of Athens. A Roman general had captured an Athenian philosopher and had told him that he meant to put him to death. The Athenian didn't seem very disturbed and so the Roman thought that probably he didn't understand. And so he said to the Athenian that maybe he didn't know what it meant to die. The Athenian said that he thought he understood it better than the Roman did. And then he said to the Roman, "Thou dost not know what it means to die, for thou dost not know what it means to live. To die is to begin to live. It is to end all stale and weary work to begin a nobler and a better. It is to leave deceitful knaves for the society of gods and goodness."

And it has been said that the most important event in life is death. We live to die and then we die to live. Death is a kind of graduation day for life. It is our only means of entrance to our eternal lives. And it seems to me to be a very helpful procedure to spend a little time preliving our death. That is, what kind of person would you like to be when the last hour of your life arrives?

The last hour is the key hour. That is the hour that judges all of the other hours. No one can tell whether or not his life has been successful until his last hour. As Sophocles said, "We must wait till evening to know how pleasant the day has been."

Certainly no one could write the life story of Jesus of Nazareth or Judas Iscariot without knowing what happened during their last hour. And I would like to tell you about some of the things that one man thought about during his last hour. This is the old legendary story of Faust. Dr. John Faust died in Wittenberg, Germany, in the year 1540. But twenty-four years before his death, he sold his soul to Satan. He said to Satan, "If you will aid me for twenty-four years, punishing my enemies and helping my friends, at the end of that time, I will forever deliver up my soul."

Now at that time that seemed like a good idea to Faust. Twenty-four years was a long time. Twenty-four years may last forever. And anyway, what difference did it make what happened after twenty-four years? But Satan, with better perspective, said, "I will wait on Faustus while he lives and he shall buy my service with his soul."

And then the twenty-four years began, and Faust had every experience of good and bad. But almost before he was aware, it was said to Faust as it must be said to everyone of us, "Thine hour is come." Now this is the first time that he had ever thought about the consequences of what he was doing. Only now did he discover how badly he had cheated himself. Then he wanted to revoke the bargain, but that was impossible. And then he prayed and he said, "Oh God, if thou canst have no mercy on my soul, at least grant some end to my incessant pain. Let Faustus live in hell a thousand years or even an hundred thousand, but at last be saved!"

But he knew that, according to his own bargain, even this could never be. And then during his last hour he sat and watched the clock tick off the seconds and finally, just as the hour struck, the last words of Faust before he died were: "Faustus is gone to hell!"

Now if Faust had lived his last hour first, he never would have permitted himelf to come to this unprofitable place. I have a relative who, when she reads a novel, always reads the last chapter first. She wants to know before she begins where she is going to be when she gets through. And that is a pretty good idea for life.

Now I don't know what it would be like if we sometime discovered that we had missed the goal of life and had allowed ourselves to become only telestial souls. I do know that it would be as far below the celestial as the twinkle of a tiny star is below the blaze of the noonday sun. We know quite a lot about the celestial kingdom. We know that that is the place which God has prepared for those who are valiant in his service and keep all of his commandments. We know quite a lot about celestial beings, as we have had a number of them appear to us upon this earth. And each time they have come, those who have received them have said that they are impossible to describe.

When the Prophet Joseph Smith had his vision of the Father and the Son, he said, "[Their] brightness and glory defy all description." (Joseph Smith—History 1:17.) That is, we don't have any background of knowledge; there isn't a vocabulary to use in describing a celestial accomplishment.

There are some things that we can't describe even in this life. For example, if I tried to describe to you the look in my little granddaughter's eyes on Christmas morning, when she's radiant and expectant and something is shining out through her face, I might have difficulty telling you about it even though I can understand it. I might try by saying she has a light in her eye, or her face beams, or her countenance is aglow. Now none of those things are true, actually. Her eyes are the same color, the same shape, the same size as they were before. But something is shining out through her face that is indescribable.

The Prophet Joseph Smith tried to describe the resurrected Jesus as he saw him in the Kirtland Temple on April 3, 1836. And he said, "His eyes were as a flame of fire." (D&C 110:3.) It isn't a twinkle anymore; I suppose it is now magnified a few million times. I suppose that actually there wasn't any fire there at all, any more than there is a light in my granddaughter's eyes. He is trying to describe something which can't be described. He said, "His face shown above the brightness of the sun"; and that is pretty bright!

We sometimes imagine that Jesus is different than we are, but the Prophet Joseph Smith tried to describe his some fifteen or sixteen visits with the angel Moroni. Moroni was a soldier who lived upon our continent. For the last thirty-seven years of his life he lived alone. He said, "My father hath been slain [as well as] all my kinsfolk, and I have not friends nor whither to go." "Wherefore," said he, "I wander whithersoever I can for the safety of mine own life." (Mormon 8:5, Moroni 1:3.)

He didn't have a warm bathroom to go into every morning or someone to get him a good breakfast or provide him with clean clothing. We might imagine that during these many long and lonely years he had allowed his personality to run down a little bit. And then we see him for the last time as he stood there on the edge of his grave, writing us his last paragraph. In closing his great book he said, "And now I bid unto all, farewell. I soon go to rest in the paradise of God, until my spirit and body shall again reunite, and I am brought forth triumphant through the air, to meet you before the pleasing bar of the great Jehovah, the Eternal Judge of both quick and dead." (Moroni 10:34.)

And then there followed a long silence of fourteen centuries. For 1,403 years we heard nothing more, until on the night of September 21, 1823, this same old man, now resurrected and glorified, stood by the bedside of Joseph Smith. And the Prophet tried to describe him as he then appeared. And while he said that was impossible, yet he tried. And here are some of the phrases he used. He said, "His whole person was glorious beyond description, and his countenance truly like lightning." (Joseph Smith—History 1:32.) Not only was his person glorious, but even his clothing was brilliant. "Beyond anything earthly I had ever seen," said he, "nor do I believe that any earthly thing could be made to appear so exceedingly white and brilliant." (Joseph Smith—History 1:31.)

We all know the things that we do to make this body a pleasant habitation. We bathe it and keep it clean; we dress it in the most appropriate clothing. Sometimes we ornament it with jewelry. If we're very wealthy we buy necklaces and bracelets and diamond rings and other things to make this body sparkle and shine and make it a pleasant place. Sometimes we work on it a little bit with cosmetics and eyebrow tweezers. Sometimes we don't help it very much, but we keep working at it all the time.

Now if you think it would be pleasant to be dressed in expensive clothing, what do you think it would be like sometime to be dressed in an expensive body—one that shines like the sun, one that is beautiful beyond all comprehension, with quickened senses, amplified powers of perception, and vastly increased capacity for love, understanding, and happiness. And we might just keep in mind that God runs the most effective beauty parlor ever known in the world.

Socrates was a very homely man, and he prayed to the Lord and said, "Make me beautiful within." We have all seen plain people who have been made beautiful by the working of a radiant spirituality. A godly spirit will make the plainest body beautiful. Great mental and spiritual qualities transform our bodies into their likeness.

And so we come back to the place where we began. What a thrilling experience that we may live well, enabling us to die well and then live with God in the celestial kingdom throughout eternity. The apostle Paul said, we die, "and, behold, we live." (2 Corinthians 6:9.)

And I would like to repeat the prayer of a very thoughtful man who said, *"Great God, I ask thee for no meaner pelf / Than that I may not disappoint myself."* (Thoreau, "A Prayer.")

And may God bless us, everyone, that we may magnify our callings and our opportunities. For this I sincerely pray in the name of Jesus Christ. Amen.

Come Now!

Richard L. Evans

A thought suggested by Dr. Lindsay Curtis expresses well the summons all of us will sometime receive from the Great Judge and Father of us all: "Come as you are . . . but come *now!*" (*Thoughts for 2 ½ Minute Talks*, Bookcraft, 1966.) It is a profound thought to ponder—the readiness of any or all or each of us to face any eventuality. Sometimes we can straighten out our lives, straighten out the record, finish our unfinished business, arrange our disordered affairs and make amends—*if* we have time. But we don't always have time. Many centuries ago Cicero said: "No man can be ignorant that he must die, nor be sure that he may not this very day." This is true of all of us. Illness, accident, unforeseen events—"No man can be . . . sure that he may not [die] this very day."

And so, to use a well-worn phrase, we simply ought to be prepared. We ought to be doing what we should be doing. We should be at peace with ourselves and with our loved ones and with all others also. We should have our desks, our documents, our debts, our affairs in order. We should clean out the grudges and the grievances, the feuds, if any, with those who are near us and with those far from us. If we do, come what may, when it may, we will be ready; and in the meantime, we will be much more effective and efficient, and every day will be more peaceful, more productive. A person at peace with himself and with

"The Spoken Word" from Temple Square, presented over KSL and the Columbia Broadcasting System January 8, 1967. Copyright 1967. Reprinted in *Improvement Era*, March 1967, p. 76.

those he lives and works with simply lives a better, happier life. Quarreling, dragging around unfinished business, delinquent obligations, unresolved differences, strained relationships, a sense of error, a sense of guilt, a sense of not having faced up to facts, tend to clutter and tarnish the living of life. It isn't easy to face facts, but it isn't easy not to. And letting unfinished and undone things and unhappy feelings and unresolved obligations always hang over us is too heavy a load.

"Come as you are . . . but come *now!*" When we receive this summons, we'll be on our way; and we ought to be ready for it, and at such peace with ourselves and with other people that we can enjoy each day, each hour, each opportunity, whenever the call comes. Come now—just as you are.

Brigham Young's Last Will and Testament

I, Brigham Young, wish my funeral services to be conducted in the following manner:

When I breathe my last I wish my friends to put my body in as clean and wholesome state as can conveniently be done, and preserve the same for one, two, three or four days, or as long as my body can be preserved in a good condition. I want my coffin made of plump $1\frac{1}{4}$ inch boards, not scrimped in length, but two inches longer than I would measure, and from two to three inches wider than is commonly made for a person of my breadth and size, and deep enough to place me on a little comfortable cotton bed, with a good suitable pillow for size and quality; my body dressed in my temple clothing, and laid nicely into my coffin, and the coffin to have the appearance that if I wanted to turn a little to the right or to the left, I should have plenty of room to do so. The lid can be made crowning.

At my interment I wish all of my family present that can be conveniently, and the male members wear no crepe on their hats or on their coats; the females to buy no black bonnets, nor black dresses, nor black veils; but if they have them they are at liberty to wear them. The services may be permitted, as singing and a prayer offered, and if any of my friends wish to say a few words, and really desire, do so; and when they have closed their services, take my remains on a bier, and repair to the little burying ground, which I have reserved on my lot east of the White House on the hill, and

From Richard H. Cracroft and Neal E. Lambert, *A Believing People; Literature of the Latter-day Saints*, Brigham Young University Press, 1974, pp. 110-11.

in the southeast corner of this lot, have a vault built of mason work large enough to receive my coffin, and that may be placed in a box, if they choose, made of the same material as the coffin—redwood. Then place flat rocks over the vault sufficiently large to cover it, that the earth may be placed over it—nice, fine, dry earth—to cover it until the walls of the little cemetery are reared, which will leave me in the southeast corner. This vault ought to be roofed over with some kind of temporary roof. There let my earthly house or tabernacle rest in peace, and have a good sleep, until the morning of the first resurrection; no crying or mourning with anyone as I have done my work faithfully and in good faith.

I wish this to be read at the funeral, providing that if I should die anywhere in the mountains, I desire the above directions respecting my place of burial to be observed; but if I should live to go back with the Church to Jackson County, I wish to be buried there.

> Brigham Young
> November 9th, 1873,
> Salt Lake City, Utah.

Brigham Young's wishes were carried out to the letter, following his death on August 28, 1877.

Section 3

The Death of a Loved One

A Weeping Eye Can Never See

Elaine Cannon

The death of a husband is a sorrowful, personal experience. There are ways to sublimate such a separation or to take the sting out of it. Even the passage of time can blunt death's sharp edges. But only ultimate reunion can assuage it. The partners in a celestial marriage know they'll be reunited some day. So it's more than mere comfort that's needed when the trial of supreme loneliness comes; it is direction for living without being more lonely than one can bear, a method for arriving at peace and keeping hope in one's heart.

Each woman must rise to the challenge in her own way. Here is how the wives of deceased General Authorities have come to terms with sorrow and how they go about making life meaningful and rich.

Count Your Many Blessings

"My world seemed shattered when my husband died suddenly in his sleep," recalls Elva Cowley, widow of Elder Matthew Cowley of the Council of the Twelve. "I had always loved the out-of-doors, but even the sky seemed dim to me on a sunny day. I'd look at people and wonder how they could walk down the street smiling."

That was in 1953, and Sister Cowley has lived to say, "Death of a loved one is sweet compared to some of the things people go through in life. I learned this soon enough while working at the Primary Children's Hospital—the job

From *Ensign*, May 1973, pp. 41-47.

that was the beginning of my finding joy in life again."

Shortly after Elder Cowley's funeral, Sister Elva faced up to the fact that she must not sit and mope and feel sorry for herself any longer. She had an adopted son to rear and a life to do something with. She accepted an executive position at the Primary Children's Hospital, where she quickly noted differences in how parents of stricken children deal with heartbreak and death.

"Some people can take things, learn a lesson from them, but some just buckle under. I remember the day a young mother came in with the most pitifully deformed baby I'd ever seen and said to me, 'I know that my Heavenly Father loves me because he knew he could send this little spirit to me and that I would love it and care for it.' Well," Sister Cowley continues, "that was the day I began counting my blessings. Such a store of them—proving that the Lord loved me, too. I knew I must not give in to the negativism that Satan tempts us with."

The Cowleys were great collectors. Their apartment is filled with interesting items from all over the world. There is the special display holding Elder Cowley's amazing collection of Royal Doulton jugs and unusual items from the Maori culture he came to love during his New Zealand assignments. Every trip they took touring missions and visiting the Saints around the world is vividly recalled now by Sister Cowley as she looks at each piece in terms of the place and the circumstances under which it was obtained.

"At first it hurt to have these things around me, but now it's a comfort. They are like a diary, a record of our sacred, special experiences with the Saints. Being alone isn't so dreadful when you have a lot to remember."

Sister Cowley, a petite and pretty, young-looking woman, believes in keeping busy. She is a temple worker and is associated with the diamond department of a department store. "If you hit the bottom of the barrel, the demands of a busy life can force you to the top again," she declares.

Be an Example of the Believer

"There is only one way to conquer the terrible agony of

being a widow, and that's to live the gospel; then the Lord will give you his peace." Thus speaks Anna Marie Critchlow, whose husband, William J., Jr., was an Assistant to the Council of the Twelve until his death in 1968.

The Critchlows had a relationship of forty-four years that was like something out of a fine romantic novel. They had been sweethearts since the day they first met at a Sunday School outing when she was seventeen and already a stake genealogical expert.

A lifetime of midday meals together—just the two of them because they enjoyed each other's company so much—is one of the things Sister Critchlow misses most now. But there are their three children and many grandchildren rallying about her to see to her every need and delight.

Sister Critchlow is a serene, queenly woman whose gentleness and refinement are matched by her appreciation of the gifts of the priesthood. Says she, "All my life I've been thankful for the priesthood, and now that I'm alone it is even more valuable. I urge the woman whose heart has been torn by separation from her beloved husband to find help when she needs it through the healing ordinances of the priesthood. The loneliness is still there," she adds, "but your heart is at peace. I recall when I was just nine years old and suffering from spinal meningitis; the doctors said I'd never walk, talk, or see again if I did recover from that severe illness. I learned then that priesthood power is greater than the finest physician. I was given a blessing, and the problems the doctors had predicted for me were wiped away. I have always turned to the priesthood in my time of need."

She seldom misses a general conference session or a Brigham Young University devotional broadcast on television, and she always goes to Sunday School to learn yet more about the gospel, because "you can't live it if you don't know it."

"If ever I am tempted to feel sorry for myself, I think of my grandmother Jeppson, who was left a widow at age forty-two with eleven unmarried children and no welfare or insurance money to help," Sister Critchlow recalls. How great a web of comfort may be drawn out of another's heart and into our own, especially from one who is an example of the believer!

Say the Good Word

The title of the book Ida Murdock Kirkham prepared and had published just three months after the death of her husband, President Oscar A. Kirkham of the First Council of the Seventy, is *Say the Good Word*. It could also be the title of their life story.

"Whether in disappointment or widowhood, one must remember to put oneself last and bring joy into the hearts of others. It is the core of the gospel," explains Sister Kirkham. Her husband died in 1958, and she has carried on their tradition of sharing scriptures and inspirational thoughts at every opportunity. Writing a special scripture on a little card and sending it to a friend in need has brought help to many, many people.

She is a great and courageous lady who honored her husband's wishes to "keep the good word alive"; with the help of her daughter, Grace Burbidge, she began the collection of thoughts for the book immediately following President Kirkham's funeral. Waiting until one feels happier, or is over the grief, isn't as wise as spreading sunshine, according to Sister Kirkham. "Then you'll feel some of your own." And in her recent serious illness, back came the "bread cast upon the water"—flowers, cards, and countless friends.

During their life together the Kirkhams were both busy—he the beloved missionary and Scout leader and she a president of the Daughters of Utah Pioneers. She serves still on the DUP advisory board. This common interest in serving and "sharing the good word" bound them together firmly.

Shortly before his death, the family gathered for a celebration of an anniversary. Sister Kirkham had prepared a scripture card, and President Kirkham led them in a family prayer and gave a father's blessing. This sacred memory is remembered by this scripture written on the card: "The Lord bless thee, and keep thee: The Lord make his face shine upon thee, and be gracious unto thee: The Lord lift up his countenance upon thee, and give thee peace." (Numbers 6:24-26.)

Meet the Trial of Your Faith

Alice Thornley Evans, wife of the late Elder Richard L. Evans of the Council of the Twelve, held up an impressively worn Triple Combination and said, "Let me read to you from Ether 12:6: '. . . wherefore, dispute not because ye see not, for ye receive no witness until after the trial of your faith.' Losing the husband you've loved for so long is the ultimate trial of one's faith, I now know. This matter of faith is all you have to fall back on at such a time. We've taught our four sons the importance of an abiding faith. I've given little talks and borne my testimony about faith. Then, out of the blue, a year ago, my big test came with Richard's death. The most helpful thing in this tremendously difficult period of adjustment has been my sure knowledge that Richard, like Christ, lives! I don't know what people do without this faith."

Theirs is a home of sweet spirit. It is full of books, music, and the fragrance of good things to eat. The telephone rings constantly with friends "checking on Alice," and grandchildren or busy sons drop by for a snack and a visit. In the midst of great sorrow, there is an aura of love and faith that comforts the friends who call to comfort.

Richard L. Evans was an important man in the world as well as the Church. His "beloved Alice" had given up a promising career as a violinist to support him in his pressing assignments. Now hers is the task of dealing with ninety big boxes of his personal files. Publishers and recording companies press with deadlines. And though a heart is sad, the work must be done.

"Work is a blessing," counsels Alice Evans. "And 'faith without works is dead,' as the scriptures say. One doesn't merely speak of beliefs; one applies them to life's problems. Like Paul said, 'I can do all things through Christ Jesus who strengtheneth me.' So when Richard died and my life-style changed, I picked up the pieces and moved on to something else."

A General Authority and his wife are in a position to see that people have problems—even people who look as if they have the world by the proverbial tail. So Sister Alice Evans spends a good part of her time sharing her marvelous warmth and goodness in careful concern for people with problems, especially widows and the single woman. "When I think of the circle of love I've lived in," comments Sister Evans, "and compare my loneliness now to that of the older, unmarried woman, I know that her problem is worse than mine. I suppose there are many ways we have our faith tested. It is up to each of us to meet that trial of our faith."

Sing a Fast Song

"When I was a young girl I'd stand at the dishpan and warble," laughed wonderful LaRue Longden, former member of the YWMIA general presidency and wife of the late Elder John Longden, Assistant to the Council of the Twelve. "Mother would listen for a time and then invariably she'd call out to me, 'Sing a fast song, LaRue,' and I'd try to oblige. It's as though I can hear her saying that to me now when I get feeling depressed or terribly alone. You may cry sometime at night, but when you're with people and the sun is up and life is moving on, you should act like a happy, believing Saint. Besides, I wouldn't dare mourn too much or Jack would haunt me!"

This delightful "lady of light" has won friends and admiration during her life of leadership because of her positive attitude and sparkling wit. She is no stranger to death, but she learned long ago that activity and attitude are the secrets of survival in times of personal tragedy.

Her first bout with death came when Elder Longden was a young bishop and she was president of the ward MIA. Their first child was just three and desperately ill in the hospital. The Longdens were on their knees when the call came telling them of her death. At the funeral Sister Longden remembers the wise counsel Elder Adam S. Bennion of the Council of the Twelve gave. He said that there are two roads one can take at a time of losing a loved one. One has a gate marked Despair; it swings open easily.

The other gate is marked Peace, and one has to struggle with it to open it. The first road if taken leads to despondency and bitterness. The other, harder one is the way of peace, character, and happiness.

"After that funeral, all the MIA people, holding flowers, formed an aisle, and I, their president, had to walk past them. I knew then they were watching me and I had to live what I'd been teaching. I began then to heed Elder Bennion's counsel."

Sister Longden nursed her mother for long months before she died of cancer. Just before her death her mother said, "LaRue, lock one of your giggles in my coffin." She wanted no tragedy made out of her going back to her Heavenly Father. Some years later, the Longdens' daughter, Gail Hickman, mother of two young sons, was stricken with polio and fought the battle to restored health with the help of the priesthood and her mother's good care. "You begin to understand a bit about the plan of life when you yearn for a loved one, fasting, praying, searching the scriptures. It is wise to dwell only on the many good things that happen then, too, like the outpouring of the Spirit and the great kindnesses of friends.

"Jack's favorite subject for his sermons was on self-mastery. I used to think I knew something about the subject, until he died," adds Sister Longden.

"Self-mastery is making yourself do something you ought to do whether you want to or not. It's singing a fast song so your troubles can't catch up with you," she concludes.

Be Anxiously Engaged

" 'We ask for strength and God gives us difficulties, which make us strong; we plead for courage, and God gives danger to overcome; we ask for favors, and God gives us opportunities.' That's a quotation by Jule Johnson that I keep here by my calendar," says Sister Madelaine B. Wirthlin. "Now that I am alone I know the truth of that quotation more than ever. It is very motivating to me. I believe I am striving harder today to learn, to grow in character, and to live better than I ever have in my life before. I know

Bishop Wirthlin is preparing a place for me, and I want to be ready."

She is the widow of Bishop Joseph L. Wirthlin, former Presiding Bishop of the Church. They have five children and twenty-seven grandchildren. All those who are married have been to the temple. All of the children have filled missions and have earned their doctorate or master's degrees. "You can't deviate from gospel principles in rearing your family, and you can't deviate in meeting the trials of death and loneliness," says Sister Wirthlin.

A vibrant, strong woman, she is planning a trip to Israel this year. She believes that since there is no recall from this test of separation, one *has* to adjust, so one might as well do it gracefully. She's as busy now as she has ever been and is anxiously engaged in many a good cause.

"I have no fear of death. I believe I understand the gospel and encourage all I meet to search its truths. I look forward to the reunion with my husband. I waited for him while he filled his first mission. I have waited countless times for him over the years of his total commitment to church service. I can wait a little longer now. I miss him terribly but I am not mourning. I am a strong believer that if we live righteously, the blessings that are promised us here and hereafter will be realized.

"I appreciate the devotion my husband had to his calling and to the counsel of the Lord. I sustained him always and now he sustains me, I'm sure, while I am anxiously striving to improve myself, help my friends and family when they need me, and be supportive of good, vital causes in our land. Isn't this God's plan? Death, in and of itself, may seem final for a time, but looking beyond, one sees the whole scheme of things. Our duty is to prepare to meet our Maker ourselves. And what a reunion!"

Share the Gospel

A quaint little lady in a very modernistic home, Sister Stayner Richards will be eighty-nine years old this year. Her favorite spot is the easy chair next to the baby grand piano with a picture of her husband on it. "Lady Jane" (as she is known by her friends and family) sits like a figure in a painting surrounded by flourishing greens, a fine collection of books, and pictures of her "current missionaries." She says, "I like to have many Church books near by because then I can pick up the one that can give me the help I need at the moment." There are letters to write to the missionaries and visits from some of her devoted family. The talk is always of the gospel—some fascinating new truth she has learned that day in study or the baptism that one of the missionaries assisted with.

"People should share the truths of the gospel whether they are on missions or not. Even in their times of sorrow they should teach the gospel, because death can be the most spiritual experience of all. That way, you help others as well as yourself," explains Sister Richards.

Here is an elect lady who is so involved in bringing the gospel and goodness into the lives of others that it never occurs to her to think about her own situation. Her daily prayer list is long because she watches closely after the needs of her loved ones and friends. She still bakes nut bread or a casserole to send to an ill neighbor, a widowed friend, or a newcomer to the block. And no one calls on her without being offered something to eat.

She is a culinary expert, and during their mission tour (when her husband was a mission president in Great Britain), she'd cook for as many as fifteen people each day in the cause of sharing the gospel. It was 1949, and England was recovering from a long war. Sister Richards would have to stand in various lines for long periods of time to get the necessary groceries. But with never a complaint she did her part to help her husband in his calling as mission president, as she had when he was stake president, bishop, and busy businessman. Later he became an Assistant to the Council of Twelve, serving until his death in 1953.

"I supported him during the years of his 'trillions' of meetings, and now I feel he is supporting me," says Sister Richards. "Yes, he is very close to me. You know, heaven isn't really very far."

Therewith to be Content

"President Moyle has been gone nine years and it

doesn't get any easier," said Sister Henry D. Moyle, whose husband served in the First Presidency under President David O. McKay. "In fact, it gets harder—you just miss them so. But the Lord does send us the comfort of his Spirit to be with us, and when I am sitting alone thinking upon our most wonderful, rich life together or pondering a problem, I feel my husband close to me and my heart is full."

Alberta Moyle spoke of a powerful lesson she has learned these past nine years as she has looked back over their lifetime together and considered the blessings of today. "It is summed up in this scripture in Philippians 4:11: ". . . for I have learned, in whatsoever state I am, therewith to be content."

President and Sister Moyle had the early aim of rearing a large, righteous, happy family. They have six children and thirty-four grandchildren. "They are wonderful people, these children and grandchildren," said Sister Moyle. "I can see now the real wisdom Brother Moyle had in early encouragement and generous rewards for their achievement."

The Moyles have been greatly blessed with material means and have been most generous in bringing joy to others by sharing and caring. Bread cast upon the water does indeed come back, and now a rich family heritage, the memories of a life of service, an attentive posterity, a rare collection of paintings and art treasures from the world over fill Sister Moyle's life. These things, coupled with a firm testimony, sustain her.

Do Your Genealogy

"If you do your genealogy, you'll never be lonely again," instructs soft-spoken Margaret Wells. "I have friends I've never even met face to face that I've become acquainted with by doing research. And some of them died long before I was born!"

A widow since 1941, she began her service as a temple worker the year after her husband, Bishop John Wells of the Presiding Bishopric, died. "I feel I owe a debt to my ancestors who accepted the gospel and came to Utah. It is a choice experience and sweet satisfaction to do something for people that they can't do for themselves." She has four file drawers full of materials and nine exquisitely prepared family histories. "But the nicest thing I ever did was take care of my aged mother for seven years until she died, nearly one hundred years of age!"

Something else that is helpful in loneliness is to "plan your days ahead of time so that you have something to look forward to or something to prepare for," says Sister Wells, whose favorite hobby is drying flowers because they are "God's creation." In addition, she thinks keeping a "tidy" house and caring for one's health are the obligations of every woman.

Sister Wells, who served for twenty-seven years on the YWMIA general board and filled a mission for the Church, firmly believes that the way to happiness is to live on an even keel. "Don't regret the past or dread the future. Life is to be lived with joy." Her husband used to say to her, "Margaret, one of the things I love about you is you wake up happy every morning." She believes this to be her responsibility, as it says in Psalm 118:24: "This is the day which the Lord hath made; we will rejoice and be glad in it."

Special days are often the most trying to a widow. A forgotten birthday or no Christmas surprise can be devastating to the best intentions of courage. Sister Wells has solved that problem for herself, too. "Every birthday and Christmas I buy myself a nice gift from John to me—something I know he'd want me to have. In thirty-two years I've never felt neglected," she declares.

Since her release as a temple worker, Sister Wells has served in ward and stake genealogical programs. She goes the extra mile by helping couples and families complete their record sheets and then accompanying them to the temple. If they are lagging a bit she coaxes them along with, "Let me know when you are ready."

People can rise to magnificent heights when the precious web of association is broken by death. For women of faith, perhaps only reminders are needed after all, when tears come unbidden. The gospel is true. The answers and hope are implicit in it if only we can see them.

But a weeping eye can never see.

When a Loved One Passes Away

Reed H. Bradford

Cathleen's parents had been married several years before she was born. They had wanted a child more than they had wanted anything. They had tried to "walk up-rightly before the Lord" so that they might be worthy to be parents. They had consulted the best medical authorities and had been told there was nothing of a physiological nature to prevent them from having children. But still no child came. They were almost ready to accept the idea that they would not have a child and were considering adoption proceedings, when it was discovered that a baby was coming. You can imagine the joy that was theirs.

Cathleen was born normally and from all appearances was in excellent health. For three years she was a pride and joy to her parents, and they loved her with all their hearts. Then one day their joy turned to sorrow. They discovered that she had a rare disease for which medical science had not found a cure. Everything that could be done was done. She was administered to by righteous men of great faith. On several occasions the family fasted and prayed for her. The best medical specialists that could be found treated her. But one spring evening she quietly passed away.

"How can we best adjust to her leaving?" her parents asked. It is a question that countless individuals have asked themselves. It may not be a child that leaves us; it may be a mother, father, brother, sister, or someone else who is close to us. Perhaps it is our mate. But in any case, how we adjust

From *Instructor*, April 1964, pp. 146-48.

to such an event has a profound bearing upon life. Some people never quite seem to recover from it; sorrow becomes their constant companion. Others learn from the experience and acquire characteristics that make them a little more divine. For any of us faced with this aspect of life, perhaps the following thoughts might be useful:

Our Heavenly Father, the Savior, and the Holy Ghost are three divine personages who are vitally interested in everyone who comes to this earth. It was the Savior who said: "I will not leave you comfortless: I will come to you. . . . He that hath my commandments, and keepeth them, he it is that loveth me: and he that loveth me shall be loved of my Father, and I will love him, and will manifest myself to him." (John 14:18, 21.) If we seek His Spirit and the influence of the Holy Ghost, not only in times of sorrow, but always, we will find an abiding peace in our souls. We will experience a fulfillment of the promise of the Savior.

Death is a passing from one phase of eternity to another. Members of The Church of Jesus Christ of Latter-day Saints have the opportunity of having their family ties protected. If a man and woman are married by the proper authority of the priesthood, and if they give devotion to the principles of the Gospel, they have the promise that they and their children will be sealed to one another forever.

Alexander Graham Bell, the Scottish-American inventor, said, "When one door closes, another opens; but we often look so long and so regretfully upon the closed door that we do not see the one which has opened for us." When a loved one leaves us, it is often easy to think of the past in terms of what was but is no more. Under such circumstances, memory produces pain. But it should not be so. Life presents many other opportunities for growth and enjoyment. We must find them and partake of them.

Death makes us painfully aware of our mistakes of omission and commission with respect to those who have passed on. We wish we might have done things differently. But the past cannot be altered. Rather we would do well to look to the present day and conclude that the most mature way to honor those we love is to live in accordance with the eternal principles of the Gospel. One person has gone on, but there are many others who need us and whom we can help. If we illumine the life of just one human soul each day, we may be sure that we bring light to others whose lives he in turn may touch.

One of the purposes of this life is to be tested and to learn to live as our Heavenly Father would have us live that we may "become His sons and daughters." "If thou art called to pass through tribulation; . . . if the billowing surge conspire against thee; if fierce winds become thine enemy; . . . and all the elements combine to hedge up the way; . . . know thou, my son, that all these things shall give thee experience, and shall be for thy good. The Son of Man hath descended below them all. Art thou greater than he?" (D&C 122:5, 7-8.) One woman who suffered a long time from cancer wrote these lines shortly before her death:

"I have had an experience which I think others might like to hear. It was mine to have—but not mine to keep. . . . What I want others to know is the experience that came because of this.

"The spirit of humility was poured down upon us, and the knowledge that God is all-powerful was made known unto us. . . .

"The spirit of repentance permeated our home. We must live better, we must do better if we would expect the Lord to bless us. . . .

"The spirit of love toward each other, toward the children, and the children toward each other was felt. We must show each other every day the affection which we had for each other. Days might be numbered—love would guide us through. . . .

"And there came to us gifts of all kinds, flowers, food, and clothes (from genuine friends).

"And people say to me, 'Oh, how terrible! What an awful experience your sickness has been. You must try and forget it and start a new life.'

"It must not be that way! I never want to forget. . . . I know that the memory of it will make me a happier and a better person."[1]

If a person is young when he or she passes on, we who are left behind often ask "why?" It is a natural question, and we could find several explanations, but our knowledge may be insufficient to say: "*this* was the reason." But we can know that our Heavenly Father is just, kind, and loving. In the eternity that includes more than just this life, He provides opportunities for lasting joy.

"Thou shalt live together in love, insomuch that thou shalt weep for the loss of them that die. . . ." (D&C 42:45.) When a loved one dies, our sorrow seems like a heavy blanket pressing down upon us. But as we adjust our lives in accordance with the ways already indicated, the blanket disappears. We are able to think of the past and have feelings of gratitude in connection with the association of those who have gone on, rather than having sorrow as the dominant feeling. We can testify, as did Anne Johnson Flint:

> *God hath not promised skies always blue,*
> *Flower-strewn pathways all our lives through,*
> *God hath not promised sun without rain,*
> *Joy without sorrow, peace without pain.*
>
> *But God hath promised strength for the day,*
> *Rest for the Laborer, light on the way,*
> *Grace for the trial, help from above,*
> *Unfailing sympathy, undying love.*[2]

---

[1]Virginia Driggs Clark. Used by permission of her husband, Harold Glen Clark.

[2]Anne Johnson Flint, "What God Hath Promised": *World's Best-Loved Poems* (New York, 1927), p. 377.

"All Day We Miss Thee, Everywhere"

Richard L. Evans

Never too far from our thoughts are questions concerning the length of life, the purpose of life—life, death, loss of loved ones, the whereabouts of those who leave us, and our own inevitable leaving of those we love. These are among the most insistent questions of all time. As to those whom we have lost, those whom we may lose, and as to ourselves: "No cogent reason remains for supposing the soul dies with the body," said Dr. Arthur H. Compton. ". . . We [scientists] find strong reasons for believing that man is of extraordinary importance in the cosmic scheme. . . . It takes a lifetime to build the character of a noble man. The exercise and discipline of youth, the struggles and failures of maturity, the loneliness and tranquility of age —these make the fire through which he must pass to bring out the pure gold of his soul. Having been thus perfected, what shall Nature do with him, annihilate him? What infinite waste! As long as there is in heaven a God of love, there must be for God's children *everlasting life!*" So spoke this eminent scientist whose knowledge was full of reason and whose reason was full of faith. All of us have losses—or will have—and no matter how many friends we have, or family, the loss of one beloved one leaves always a place unfilled in our hearts, as David Macbeth Moir said it:

> *We miss thy small step on the stair;*
> *We miss thee at thine evening prayer;*
> *All day we miss thee, everywhere.*

"The Spoken Word" from Temple Square, presented over KSL and the Columbia Broadcasting System May 26, 1968. Copyright 1968. Reprinted in *Improvement Era*, August 1968, p. 35.

To you who know the loss of loved ones, to you who think upon your own time—sometime—of leaving this life: there is a place where loved ones wait, a place, a purpose, and an everlastingness of life in the real and substantive sense. God grant to each one faith and peace and purpose, and memories made sweeter by this assurance, that when we go it will not be as strangers, but to find again beloved faces, the personal presence of family and friends.

Alone Through Death

Blaine R. Porter

Most people who lose their marriage companion through death discover that they are able to make adjustments and assume responsibilities that they had previously thought were impossible. They may also find that the routines of daily life are more easily managed than they had anticipated.

But until one has had this experience, he cannot fully realize the emptiness, the void, that is present when a choice companion is no longer there to share time, experiences, plans, disappointments, and decisions. Children can consume a good deal of one's time, and friends can help, but no one can really take the place of a marriage companion.

Because death is generally such an unwelcome event, most of us do not make adequate preparation for it. However, those who can talk intelligently about what they would like to have done when they pass away not only demonstrate an element of maturity but also relieve the loved one who remains of many decisions during a time of emotional trauma.

The intensity of the bereavement crisis for the survivor is largely determined by the length of time the couple has been married, the quality of the relationship that they were able to achieve, the number and ages of children that may be still dependent upon the remaining parent, the age of the individual, and the financial, social, and emotional resources available. All of these factors significantly affect

From *Ensign*, October 1972, pp. 74-78.

the magnitude of the adjustments to be made by the survivors.

If the death of a loved one comes suddenly or unexpectedly, the immediate reaction is usually one of disbelief: "It can't be true; you must be mistaken," or "Are you sure?" These common reactions are accompanied or immediately followed by a numbing effect, during which time the person does not fully comprehend the impact that this loss will have upon his life.

Even if certain plans and instructions have been left by the departed loved one, numerous decisions still must be made regarding funeral and burial arrangements. Sometimes it may be necessary to relocate geographically. Decisions about business, professional, or vocational responsibilities must be made; and the concern and help of many friends and relatives, although usually for only a brief period of time, must be acknowledged. All of this is compounded considerably if no plans or preparations have been made for such an occurrence.

Sometimes after a death serious feelings of guilt or remorse are felt, and these may linger on for months or even years. The remaining spouse may feel responsible in some way for the death of his companion. For example, one husband who was driving at the time of an automobile accident in which his wife was killed felt that if he had been more careful, it would not have happened, and that he was responsible not only for her death and the loss of his companion, but also for depriving the children of the presence of their mother.

Another woman, who was having a problem with one of the children at home, called her husband at work and asked him if he could come to assist. He was killed in an accident on the way home. She felt that if she had managed the problem herself and had not asked him to come, the accident would not have happened.

Some persons have mistakenly felt that the loss of their loved one was the result of their being taken by God as a punishment to the remaining spouse, who had not been living as righteously as he should.

Others who have lost loved ones may torment

themselves by trying to find explanations for their loss. The answers they find are frequently related to their religious understanding, the depth of their convictions, their skill in rationalizing, and their need to have answers for all of life's consequences. Friends and relatives usually feel free to provide answers and interpretations, but these don't always provide encouragement to the mourner.

An individual who is experiencing feelings of guilt and continued remorse should seek help from a bishop and/or a professional person who can assist and provide guidance in working through the problems. While there may be justification sometimes for such feelings, the issue should be resolved so that one's future is not mortgaged to the past.

The desire to help someone who has lost a companion is common, but knowing how best to extend that help is not so widely understood. We sometimes wonder whether we should avoid the subject. If it is brought up by ourselves or someone else, many of us are not sure how we should deal with it. In most instances the best rule to follow is to let the bereaved person determine whether or not he wishes to talk about the matter. If he does wish to talk about it, then you can probably extend the most help by being a good listener. Too often, instead of listening, the "helpful friend" feels a compulsion to share his experiences or those of someone else he has known, which doesn't really help the bereaved person.

If the survivor can set the pace and can determine when and if the issue is to be discussed and for how long and in what context, then he probably will have the kind of experience he needs and is seeking. If he wants advice, counsel, or the benefit of your experience, let him ask for it. In such a case, respond briefly; and if he wants to know more, let him pursue it.

It may be that what he needs and wants most is time to be alone to reflect, to relive pleasant memories, to work through in his own mind various alternatives that are available to him, and to select the one that seems most appropriate and desirable. It may be difficult for him to do this when he has the responsibility of entertaining a friend or relative. It may merely complicate his task if others are there sharing their experiences and giving advice and counsel.

Without intending to, we may give the impression that if our help or advice is not accepted, we will be hurt or offended. In most instances it is best to extend an offer to help and then to give it when and if it is needed and wanted. At the time of death, friends and relatives are more available to share their attention, their time, and their sympathy; but generally they return quickly to their normal activities, and in two or three weeks the one who is experiencing bereavement is left alone. That is usually the time when he most needs and wants to talk to someone.

It is common for a person who has lost a loved one to reflect upon past times they have shared and to perhaps regret that there was not a more open show of affection or that thoughtful little things he would like to have done were postponed until it was too late.

Reflecting on the loss of a companion can provide a stimulus to help one carefully evaluate his life and sometimes reorder his priorities. Often we don't appreciate things as much as we should until they are lost or until their existence is threatened.

Once a person goes through the process of evaluating his life and perhaps changing his priorities and establishing resolutions or making new commitments, he finds that it serves as a means of helping him improve the quality of his life. This is not a matter in which one makes up for deficiencies of the past or can do something for the loved one who is departed, but it does mean that he can make the remaining days and years of his life more meaningful and useful so that he is better prepared to meet his loved one when they are reunited for the rest of eternity.

A person's faith is often tested in the experience of bereavement. Even a strong testimony is put to the test when one faces a crisis such as death, and it may not be as strong as had been supposed. Some people blame God or become bitter toward the Church because they cannot see any logical or justifiable reason for their loved one's death. Others find that they have a greater resource to call upon to assist them in a time of crisis than they realized. Those who are close to the Lord and who call upon him find a deeper meaning than ever before in the beatitude that states, "Blessed are they that mourn: for they shall be comforted." (Matthew 5:4.)

An outpouring of love from God, family, and friends may not only sustain one during a difficult period; it may also strengthen one's testimony and deepen his understanding of the gospel. He may realize more fully that God does answer prayers and that he does assist us in facing the challenges and tasks that confront us.

The competence with which one deals with crises such as death depends primarily upon adaptability and flexibility. A crisis tests a person's inner resources and those outside himself that will enable him to cope with his responsibilities and opportunities. He may discover a deeper understanding of the statement of the Lord to Joseph Smith, who, in a period of trial and suffering, was told, ". . . know thou, my son, that all these things shall give thee experience, and shall be for thy good." (D&C 122:7.) And during the Prophet's same period of confinement in Liberty Jail the Lord said, "My son, peace be unto thy soul; thine adversity and thine afflictions shall be but a small moment; And then if thou endure it well, God shall exalt thee on high. . . ." (D&C 121:7-8.)

Being separated by death does not carry the social stigma that sometimes accompanies divorce, but it presents many of the same challenges, and it requires some of the same adjustments. With the loss of a marriage partner, an adjustment must be made in a person's pattern of reciprocal love and affection. There is an added responsibility of trying to fulfill the roles of both parents, and there is a need to find informal social groups for one who is now single.

While most married friends will continue to include the widowed person in social activities, it is not always easy for the single person to feel comfortable in such situations. More often it is necessary to make new friends within a different social circle. However, continuing one's association with previously established married friends is much easier in the case of bereavement than in the case of divorce. Often in the latter instance, friends feel the need to choose sides when there has been serious conflict between those who have been divorced.

Few women who are widowed are financially independent, so major adjustments may include obtaining employment or returning to school in order to be trained for employment. Arrangements must be made for the care of any children at home while the mother is working. Thus, it is important for couples who are still together to make plans for the future so that if necessary, the woman can be relatively financially independent, at least until the children are grown. It would be wise for all married couples to seek competent financial counseling on these matters.

Another major responsibility of one who suddenly finds himself in the situation of being a single parent is to adjust to changing roles in the family. It is not easy and in some ways not possible for one person to be both a father and a mother. Most of the physical needs of children at home, at school, or at church can be met or arranged for by a single parent. However, trying to meet the emotional needs of children is a different matter and sometimes results in undesirable consequences for both child and parent.

Children who are in their late teens or older usually have established their own identity and are able to face the reality of the loss of a parent with considerable poise and maturity. Younger children, however, need a great deal of help in interpreting the event and in making the adjustment. While children are usually very resilient and deserve more credit than they are often given, it is important for them to have both male and female models with whom they can identify and relate. It would be beneficial for the children if a close friend, relative, home teacher, or youth group leader could serve occasionally in the role of a substitute parent.

A widowed parent must not seek to selfishly and unrealistically meet his own needs through a child or through his children. There are many examples of this folly: the widow who turns to her son and wrecks him with her emotional demands; the widower who expects the oldest daughter of the family to take over the role of being a mother for the other children. (To some extent this experience could be a growing one for a girl in her late teens, but it has the danger of being perpetuated to the exclusion of possible educational experiences away from home, of healthy relationships with persons her own age, and of her marrying at an appropriate time.)

The single parent should take frequent inventory of his needs and those of his children who are still at home and determine whether these needs are being met with a reasonable degree of success and without undue imposition on any family member. Some single parents mistakenly make sacrifices for what they believe will be in the best interests of their children.

In order for a person to remain emotionally, physically, and spiritually healthy and to be very much alive and involved in the world, it is also necessary that some of his own needs be met. The parent who is always sacrificing for his children may become an unhappy, poorly adjusted person who is not able to function effectively.

Remarriage is a possibility for almost all single parents and is highly probable for many, but there are some differences between the widow and the widower. Remarriage for the widower is the respectable and even the expected thing. Twice as many widowers as widows remarry during the first five years after their spouse's death, and this ratio maintains for the next nine or ten years. Whether this is due to a greater opportunity for men to contract a second marriage or to a fundamental difference between the sexes is difficult to determine. Certainly a higher proportion of widows to widowers is a determining factor in the smaller number of widows who remarry.

It also seems to be more acceptable and more common for a man to marry a woman substantially younger than he is or who has not previously been married than it is for a widow to marry someone younger or one who has not been previously married.

Another factor that may prevail is that a woman may be more willing to accept the emotional responsiblities of helping rear another woman's children than her male counterpart would be in a similar situation.

A father with several young children who have lost

their mother may feel that it is urgent to find a woman who can come into the home and be a mother to his children and help him with the responsibilities of rearing them. This sometimes puts pressure on a widower to move into marriage more quickly and less cautiously than he should. While the immediate needs of the children are important, he still should be choosing wisely not only a temporary mother for his children but a companion for himself.

It is taken for granted in many social groups that a young widow will remarry rather quickly. Many friends and relatives are quite anxious to assume the role of matchmaker, making frequent offers to arrange for introductions to eligible marriage partners. Conversely, some relatives may communicate to a son-in-law or a daughter-in-law that he or she would be disloyal to the family or would not be paying proper respect to the departed spouse by marrying again or by remarrying within a short period of time.

Some people find it difficult, if not impossible, to enter into another marriage relationship because they feel that they are being untrue to their departed companion. Each individual has the responsibility and should have the privilege of making the decision of whether or not he will marry, but it is certainly not a decision to be made hastily and without careful consideration.

It is not unusual to idolize the first mate. This is more true of women than of men. The idolized image of a dead mate, an image to which no living man could measure up, is an important deterrent to remarriage for many widows. Such idolization can create either a barrier for remarriage or serious problems in case of remarriage.

The single parent with children who considers remarriage must also cope with their feelings and attitudes. Usually, at first, children will not want their parents to remarry. As they grow older, however, and as the time extends from the loss of the other parent, they may be more amenable to the thought of their father or mother marrying again. Each parent who loses a companion should consider the possibility of remarriage, with the criteria being the best interest of all concerned.

Many widows and widowers will not have the opportunity to remarry. However, for them life can still be rich, full, and rewarding. Each day presents many opportunities for self-growth, for service to others, for increasing the Godlike qualities for which we are striving, for preparing ourselves to be reunited with our companion and returning to the presence of our Father in heaven.

One of the realities of losing a loved one through death is experiencing feelings of loneliness. Most people do not understand the phenomenon of loneliness; they usually try to escape from it rather than capitalize upon it. Loneliness is neither good nor bad, but is a point of intense and timeless awareness of the self, a beginning that initiates totally new sensitivities and awarenesses and that can result in bringing a person deeply in touch with his own existence and with others in a more fundamental sense than has ever occurred before.

Experiencing solitude gives one the opportunity to draw upon untouched capacities and resources. It can bring into awareness new dimensions of self, new beauty, new power for human compassion, and a reverence for the precious nature of each breathing moment.

In solitary moments, man experiences truth, beauty, nature, reverence, humanity. Loneliness enables one to return to a life with others with renewed hope and vitality, with fuller dedication, with a deeper desire to come to a healthy resolution of problems and issues involving others, and with the possibility and hope for a rich, true life with others. Our task, then, is to learn to care for our own loneliness and suffering and for the loneliness and suffering of others. By this means, one can gain strength and growth in new directions to enhance his dignity, maturity, beauty, and capacity for tenderness and love.

The Latter-day Saint understanding of eternal marriage is one of the most important sources of comfort for one who has lost a companion and who feels worthy of having the marriage continue for eternity. The death is looked upon as a temporary separation, and one can look forward to being reunited with his loved one. While death is almost always an unwelcomed event, it is much more tolerable when one has the assurance of being reunited with his loved ones.

Death separates some who have not been sealed for eternity. A surviving spouse, in such a case, has the opportunity of preparing for an eternal marriage with the departed one or with some other worthy individual.

We no doubt knew before we were born that we were coming into a world that would include joys and sorrows, pain and comfort, peace and hardship, health and sickness, success and disappointment. We knew also that someday we would die. If we accepted the privilege of coming to this world with these risks involved, it is our duty now to accept with faith consequences that are beyond our control and take hope in the reunion that will surely come.

And What of Death?

Richard L. Evans

Some of the loneliest of loneliness in life comes with the loss of loved ones, and some of the most sobering concern comes with wondering where they are and when we again shall see them. Moved by such searching thoughts, Andrew Jackson said: "Heaven will not be heaven to me if I do not meet my wife there." Heaven to be heaven must have within it that which makes of heaven a wonderfully happy home—with loved ones as a part of all that makes completeness in an everlastingness of life. How could it be otherwise? How could all this order, all this beauty—the earth, the sky, the sea, the glory of spring, the magnificent succession of all seasons, the love of life, the love of loved ones, the endless evidence of Providence, of plan, of purpose, the mind and memory of man—how could all this be other than eternal and of personal continuance? "When I consider the wonderful activity of the mind," said Cicero, "so great a memory of what is past, and such capacity for penetrating the future; when I behold such a number of arts and sciences, and such a multitude of discoveries . . . I believe and am firmly persuaded that a nature which contains so many things within itself cannot but be immortal." "Seems it strange that thou shouldst live forever?" asked Edward Young. "Is it less strange that thou shouldst live at all?" Life is the miracle, and that it should be always is no more a miracle than that it is at all. And so the mean-

"The Spoken Word" from Temple Square, presented over KSL and the Columbia Broadcasting System April 6, 1969. Copyright 1969. Reprinted in *Improvement Era*, June 1969, p. 123.

ing, the message of this moment: that He who gave us birth and life and loved ones has given us also the limitless possibilities of everlasting life. And what of death?

> *Ay! it will come, —the bitter hour!—but bringing*
> *A better love beyond, more subtle-sweet;*
> *A higher road to tread, with happier singing,*
> *And no cross-ways to part familiar feet!*
> —Edwin Arnold, "The New Lucian"

Easing the Sting of Death

James A. Cullimore

Understanding the gospel and the plan of salvation can greatly ease the sting of death. Knowing the beauty of God's plan for the salvation of his children sometimes makes even death beautiful. We understand that death is a very necessary part of the great plan of salvation and that it is the means of the separation of the body and the spirit, in which the spirit returns to God and the body returns to the earth. As the scripture says, "Then shall the dust return to the earth as it was: and the spirit shall return unto God who gave it." (Ecclesiastes 12:7.)

Death is just as necessary as birth in this great plan. Birth into this life is the means by which the spirit and the body are joined together for their great mission on this earth. Resurrection is the process whereby the spirit, which separated from the body in death, is again reunited with the body, which has been purified, glorified, and immortalized, never to be separated again.

Yes, even death can be beautiful as we understand the plan of the Lord and know that in life we have lived well. Even the pangs of sorrow, because of separation and the many memories, are momentarily overshadowed by this understanding.

I shall never forget one such beautiful occasion. My parents had lived a good life. They had celebrated their sixty-fifth wedding anniversary. To them had been born twelve children; six boys filled missions; all the family is ac-

Address delivered at the 139th Semiannual General Conference of the Church, October 1969. Published in *Improvement Era*, December 1969, pp. 78-80.

tive in the Church. Father filled a three-year mission. He was a bishop for nearly thirty years. Mother had completely sustained my father in all his Church activities and had held many responsible positions in the ward herself. When father left on his mission, they had one child and were expecting another. In her eighty-fourth year, mother broke her hip and was quite ill in the hospital. My father, at eighty-six, was still very active and drove to work each day. He came from work that day, visited with mother in the hospital for a while, then went on to the house. That evening he passed away peacefully. Mother never knew of his passing for the next day she passed away also. A double funeral was held. As we all visited during the evening of the viewing, realizing the beautiful, full lives both had lived, and knowing the kindness of the Lord in sparing either of them the loneliness of being alone, there could be no real sorrow—yes, momentary grief in separation, but otherwise beautiful peace in knowing they were together.

"Not long ago a noted scholar wrote a book entitled *The Meaning of Death.* The contents of his work were taken from several case histories of individuals who were suffering from terminal cancer. These people were faced with the immediate problem of dying.

"The object of the study was to assess the feelings of those who were about to die. Almost universally the patients agreed that the inevitability of death was not the issue. The real issue was how to live a full life. They all seemed to agree that the problem of dying is the regret of not having lived." (Max W. Swenson, "Living Life Abundantly," *Impact*, Winter 1969, p. 8.)

The concern of living a good life and keeping the commandments in preparation to meet our Maker has been the concern of mankind from the beginning. Unto Cain the Lord said, "If thou doest well, shalt thou not be accepted? and if thou doest not well, sin lieth at the door. . . ." (Genesis 4:7.)

Unto Moses the Lord gave a code of living that was reaffirmed in the meridian dispensation by the Savior and again in this dispensation in which he said:

"Thou shalt have no other gods before me.

"Thou shalt not make unto thee any graven image.

"Thou shalt not take the name of the Lord thy God in vain.

"Remember the sabbath day, to keep it holy.

"Honour thy father and thy mother.

"Thou shalt not kill.

"Thou shalt not commit adultery.

"Thou shalt not steal.

"Thou shalt not bear false witness.

"Thou shalt not covet. . . ." (See Exodus 20:2-17.)

The Lord exhorted the children of Israel to obedience when he said, "Behold, I set before you this day a blessing and a curse;

"A blessing, if ye obey the commandments of the Lord your God, which I command you this day:

"And a curse, if ye will not obey the commandments of the Lord your God. . . ." (Deuteronomy 11:26-28.)

The Savior promised, "For the Son of man shall come in the glory of his Father with his angels; and then he shall reward every man according to his works." (Matthew 16:27.)

Possibly one of the most direct answers as to proper conformity in life was given by Peter on the day of Pentecost. Filled with the Holy Ghost, he delivered a powerful sermon and bore witness to the divinity of Jesus Christ. Many were pricked in their hearts and wanted to know what they should do to be saved. He said, "Repent, and be baptized every one of you in the name of Jesus Christ for the remission of sins, and ye shall receive the gift of the Holy Ghost. For the promise is unto you, and to your children, and to all that are afar off, even as many as the Lord our God shall call." (Acts 2:38-39.)

Paul, who found the Galatian saints believing false doctrine, called them to repentance, saying, "Be not deceived; God is not mocked: for whatsoever a man soweth, that shall he also reap. For he that soweth to his flesh shall of the flesh reap corruption; but he that soweth to the Spirit shall of the Spirit reap life everlasting." (Galatians 6:7-8.)

In this dispensation the Lord has said: "If thou wilt do good, yea, and hold out faithful to the end, thou shalt be saved in the kingdom of God, which is the greatest of all the gifts of God; for there is no gift greater than the gift of salvation." (D&C 6:13.)

But the Lord has not left us alone. In every dispensation of the gospel, he has administered unto his children— instructing them as to how they can regain his presence. He walked and talked with the ancient prophets. The prophet Alma tells how the Lord sent angels to converse with men in his time and reveal the plan of redemption. ". . . he saw that it was expedient that man should know concerning the things whereof he had appointed unto them;

"Therefore he sent angels to converse with them, who caused men to behold of his glory.

"And they began from that time forth to call on his name; therefore God conversed with men, and made known unto them the plan of redemption, which had been pre-pared from the foundation of the world; and this he made known unto them according to their faith and repentance and their holy works." (Alma 12:28-30.)

Possibly one's concern about not having lived well is really in not knowing what his real purpose in life is. Real peace of mind comes from a firm conviction of the plan of salvation as revealed to us of the Lord; that we are the children of God, created in his image; that he is the Father of our spirits; that we lived with him in a glorious spiritual existence before this temporal existence; that this mortal state is probationary; that through death and the resurrec-tion, having lived a worthy life, having complied with the ordinances of the gospel, we might enter again into the presence of God. Peace comes as we know the gospel and live it, as we develop a strong testimony of its divinity, as we are vindicated by the Holy Spirit in our good works.

In this dispensation God has also visited the earth and sent his messengers to reveal unto us his plan of redemp-tion, that we may know of his will and feel his sustaining spirit as we do his bidding. He has said, ". . . Repent, repent, and prepare ye the way of the Lord, and make his paths straight; for the kingdom of heaven is at hand;

"Yea, repent and be baptized, every one of you, for a remission of your sins; yea, be baptized even by water, and then cometh the baptism of fire and of the Holy Ghost." (D&C 33:10-11.)

It is our witness to the world that the gospel of Jesus Christ, as revealed to the Prophet Joseph Smith, contains the direction and understanding of eternal life, that by abiding by its principles and teachings and by complying with its ordinances, one might have peace and satisfaction by the vindication of the spirit, and whether in life or death they will know all is well—death will have no sting.

I leave you this witness, my brothers and sisters, and witness unto you that God lives, that Jesus is the Christ, and that this is his church, in the name of Jesus Christ. Amen.

Dealing with Death
and Dying
Clifford J. Stratton

Late one summer afternoon while I was studying in my college dormitory room, I received a phone call from my best friend, Dave, and his new wife, Peggy. They were about to conclude their honeymoon and wanted to take me to a movie.

Dave and Peggy were probably my closest friends. I had introduced them to each other. We'd served together for a year on the same stake MIA board. Dave and I had corresponded during our missions, and we came back to the same school. I was a witness when Dave and Peggy were married in the temple.

"Only one catch," Peggy explained over the phone. "I get to choose your date. There is someone very special I want you to meet; she's my cousin, Marsha. . . ."

I had been so close to this couple for such a long time, and we had shared so many wonderful times together, that I readily consented to date the attractive young lady she had in mind, whom I had known for most of my life but with whom I had never become involved socially. Ten months later they accompanied us to the temple when we were married.

All four of us were overjoyed when Peggy became pregnant. Then tragedy struck. One week before their first wedding anniversary, Dave was rushed to the hospital and in a few days passed away because of a brain tumor.

Marsha and I felt the loss very deeply. In fact, this was

From *Ensign*, February 1976, pp. 45-47.

the first time in my life that I felt real grief and bereavement. I wanted very much to be able to comfort Peggy, but I simply didn't know how. I felt helpless when confronted with her pain and her questions.

Now, many years later, I have seen death and dying in my family, as a bishop, and as a doctor. I find that most members react as I did at Dave's death. We sincerely want to help but are hesitant because we are uncomfortable in our own inexperience. Each time I assist the bereaved and dying I feel that same hesitancy. Yet there are ways to help, and the value that comes from the very substantial support and strength of a sincerely concerned family member, priesthood leader, or friend cannot be measured.

Let me share with you some of the understanding I have gained about bereavement—understanding that could have made me of infinitely more assistance to Peggy, understanding that we all need in order to provide effective, compassionate service.

It is important to remember that we feel a loss at every death. We long for the touch, the sight, the presence of the one we lost, and even a secure knowledge of the plan of salvation doesn't take away the longing.

Although each loss is different, there are consistent stages of bereavement that each widow or widower seems to feel. The family member, priesthood leader, or visiting teacher can be a genuine source of help by providing the sensitive support necessary during each stage.

The first stage of grief is merciful: a numbness that comes with shock. "The numbness was a blessing," said Peggy in retrospect. "Everything inside you stops. Even after the funeral I tried to fill my life with as many activities as I could because it was a security blanket. Yet, subconsciously, I felt the loss, and my grandmother says I cried in my sleep every night during this time."

The bereaved individual goes through the daily routine like a robot. A widow takes the children to the park, cleans house, and irons clothes; a widower works, eats, and sleeps. Both are in a daze.

It may take a few days or several months, but eventually the numbness wears off and sorrow sets in.

Peggy expressed it this way: "I was overwhelmed by a sorrow that filled my whole being. The realization that Dave was gone and I was alone, really alone, deeply hurt me. With the sorrow came a flood of anxieties—the responsibility of raising an unborn child by myself, my financial situation. I felt intense sorrow and loneliness."

It is natural to feel anger accompanying the grief. Often a widow will feel that she has been cheated because her husband's influence is no longer felt in her and her family's lives. As Peggy said, bitterly, "It's not fair, when I'll have a child to raise." Occasionally, anger is even expressed against the person who is being mourned, that he "left me in this situation," as if he had a choice.

It is also natural to sometimes feel angry with God: "I really wanted to die. I wanted to go with him. I was very bitter against the Lord, even though my testimony was strong. He had taken Dave and then refused to let me go with him. I felt a very deep bitterness against the Lord."

Anger is very difficult for most comforters to deal with, but in most cases it is best to neither encourage nor discourage it. Those who mourn honestly feel angry and bitter, and to respond, "You don't know what you're saying" or "You don't really mean that" is pointless and unhelpful. It seems best not to agree with their anger or aggressively oppose it either, for it is a natural stage of bereavement.

One of the most difficult adjustments the widow or widower has to make is the change in people's attitudes. They discover that our society and the Church are, to a large extent, couple and family oriented. Peggy yearned for comfort and companionship and turned to the world of families where she used to belong so naturally, only to find that she was excluded from most of the intimacies of her old friendships. She was encouraged to seek special friends in what is now called the Special Interest group, where she had had no previous experience and had no intimate relationships. These adjustments can be difficult indeed. The word *widow* itself, which originated in the Sanskrit and means "separate" or "empty," can become harsh and painful.

In the next stage, the widow or widower wants to begin

to live a normal life and not be consumed with the past. Peggy said, "It was a hard decision to make. I wanted to fulfill my existence, my patriarchal blessing. I always knew I would have to face reality, and finally I did. There is a loneliness that never goes away, but you have to live."

During each of the foregoing stages, but more particularly during the stages of grief and anger, Peggy needed to know that people sincerely cared: "I appreciated anything that anyone did. After the numbness wore off there was nothing. No one invited me anywhere. I really felt like I was not being invited because they felt uncomfortable. But that is when I needed it most. Not words, but activity, love, and involvement."

This is the time to invite the widow or widower over for dinner, to join with your family in the park for a home evening activity, or to go to a play or movie. If a baby-sitter is needed, you make the arrangements. Don't talk about death unless the bereaved brings it up. Be normal; act natural.

And finally comes acceptance and peace of mind. The bereaved person, realizing his or her strength, becomes independent. There is more understanding and stability, and the poignant memories find their place and perspective. As new problems approach, successful resolutions become easier; life becomes happier, richer, and more enjoyable. But though the widow or widower has accepted reality, the true nature of his or her love for the departed partner has not diminished.

Recently Peggy told me, "I felt his presence for several months after he died, as if he had not gone spiritually. Then, when I began to face reality, I accepted the fact that he needed to be working at whatever he was called to do, and he left."

An equally painful situation for most of us is when a friend or family member is terminally ill.

We need to understand that the critically ill individual also experiences several distinct stages as death approaches. Such an understanding can provide a basis from which substantial support can be given in each of these stages, and which will help maintain close, eternal relationships.

Initially, the individual denies that he is critically ill: "There has been a mix-up in the records" or "The doctor has made a wrong diagnosis; I'm not sick." Often this denial persists for some time, even after several physicians have corroborated the original diagnosis. This temporary defense is usually replaced sooner or later by partial acceptance, and less radical defense mechanisms are adopted.

When the individual is no longer able to maintain his fantasy of health, he may experience feelings of anger, envy, and resentment. The individual now asks himself, "Why me?" or "Brother Jones is old; his family is all grown up. I still have much of life ahead of me. Why not him?"

This stage is one of the most difficult for the family and ward to cope with, because his anger is irrational and displaced at random. Family and friends feel his resentment and anger, and then respond either with grief and tears, or guilt and shame. It is natural to avoid future visits, but this only increases the person's discomfort and anger. It is important that the individual be respected and understood. He must be treated as a valuable human being who will be visited and listened to with pleasure, not merely from duty or assignment. If he expresses anger against Deity, the visitor should not be alarmed. These feelings are temporary, and contradicting them has no positive effect.

In the next stage, the individual hopes that God will postpone the inevitable happening. He might say, "If Heavenly Father has decided to take me from this earth and he didn't respond to my angry pleas, he may be more favorable if I am humble."

About the same time, he becomes aware of how his situation is affecting others and feels sincerely concerned about his imposition. Since extensive treatment and hospitalization usually bring heavy financial burdens, the individual usually feels sad and even guilty. If the father is ill, he sees the family income dwindle. The mother may have to work. If the mother is ill, the small children have to be given to relatives or friends for their daytime care. Family members, or church leaders if no adult relatives are available, should do all they can to help reorganize the household, since the individual's depression lifts quickly when he or she sees that these vital issues have been taken care of.

There is at this time a second type of depression, a silent type. The individual realizes his impending separation from his loved ones and mourns in much the same way as the living do after the death of a family member. All of the same human courtesies should be afforded him that we give anyone who has suffered a family loss. He should be allowed to express his sorrow, and interference from visitors who try too hard to cheer him up are inappropriate. He may silently turn to sincere, meaningful prayer and begin to think of things ahead rather than behind. He will be grateful to those who can sit with him quietly without constantly telling him not to be sad.

If the individual has had enough time and support in the initial stages of adjustment, he will enter the final stage of being neither angry nor depressed. He becomes neither happy nor sad, but is in a peaceful mood of acceptance. This is the time when the family usually needs more help and support than the person, for often they have not yet come to grips with reality.

Death is a part of God's plan and provides an opportunity for faith to overcome fear. It is a time when free agency does not allow us the option of whether or not we *will* face the trial, only *how* we will face it.

When the bereaved or terminally ill individual asks my assistance in explaining or justifying their problem, I counsel them that their primary task is not to find explanations but to *accept* death and dying. Every mourner and every terminally ill individual has to face this reality, and each comes to the task with unique spiritual and emotional characteristics and needs. Yet there are general stages, any or all of which may be observable, and the sensitive family member, priesthood leader, visiting teacher, or friend who is aware of these emotional stages is better equipped to help the individual face death and dying successfully.

The sensitive companion will not avoid discussing the person's questions, for this can be an important assistance to those who are bereaved or dying; however, he will be a listener primarily, not a preacher indulging in speculation. Receptive to the infinite experience and wisdom available through the Holy Ghost, he will quietly help the individual resolve his complex, searching questions and to come to an understanding of the importance of faith in God as a vital step in coming to acceptance.

Recently in our ward an elderly sister suffered the loss of her husband. Again I observed how members who have suffered a loss and who have a secure knowledge of the plan of salvation find their testimonies to be a substantial source of comfort and peace of mind. She did ask several of the questions that are often asked by the bereaved or dying, but she already knew the answers to most of them. The presence of a family member and friends with the same knowledge provided adequate emotional support, and this sister quickly came to understand that her husband had lived a long and fruitful life and that he was going to prepare a place for her.

On the other hand, some time ago I counseled a young Latter-day Saint widow who seemed to have an insatiable desire to know what the spirit world and life after death are like. She had to feel that her husband was personally needed in the spirit world for a specific mission. She searched the scriptures, studied Church history, and read several books that included a discussion of the spirit world. After several weeks of concentrated study, she had satisfied her need and progressed very smoothly toward acceptance. She had not found the answers to all of her questions, but she had resolved enough of them to discontinue the grieving process.

The answers the person ultimately decides upon are perhaps not critically important in and of themselves so long as they are within the gospel context. What is important in a situation where death has occurred or is inevitable is that questions are resolved to the individual's satisfaction so that he or she can continue to grow toward the stage of acceptance.

Providing service and comfort to those who have suffered a loss or who are terminally ill should not be approached with reluctance. The strength we can offer to such people in need is immeasurable, and is greatly appreciated.

If we will become educated to the needs and the moods of the bereaved and terminally ill and will allow ourselves to be receptive to the promptings of the Holy Ghost, we will not be hesitant because of our inexperience, and there will be very few situations in which we cannot be of significant help.

Trust Him to Run
All Things Well

Richard L. Evans

The swift passing of the seasons brings all of us at times to think upon the length of life, as friends and loved ones come and leave, and as we ourselves face always such uncertainties. Not one of us knows how long he will live, how long his loved ones will live. "No man can be ignorant that he must die," said Cicero, "nor be sure that he may not this very day." But beyond all this—beyond all fretting, worrying, and brooding about the length of life—there is evidence everywhere to quiet our hearts, to give us peace and faith for the future, and assurances that we can count on. Spring returned again this morning. We knew it would—and it did. And just so surely as all this, life has purpose, plan, and pattern that includes eternal continuance, with loved ones waiting. And with all sorrows, loss of loved ones, loneliness, there is this that we may know: that in a universe which runs so well, the Power who runs it well is that same Power who knows each human heart, and quiets and softens sorrow, and gives assurances we so much seek, as each day brings its undisclosed events. We come; we live; we leave. Our loved ones leave—but we and they live always and forever. Don't fret. Don't doubt. Don't cling to grieving. Don't fight life, or give up, or brood, or be bitter and rebellious, or let go of faith in the future. All of us know loneliness; all of us search ourselves, and ask for answers. Trust Him, who has done so much so well, to do all things

"The Spoken Word" from Temple Square, presented over KSL and the Columbia Broadcasting System May 31, 1970. Copyright 1970. Reprinted in *Improvement Era*, August 1970, p. 31.

well. Trust Him to bring peace and comfort and quietness and assurance to your soul inside. "Once more the Heavenly Power makes all things new." (Alfred, Lord Tennyson, "Early Spring.") This you can count on.

Children
and
Death

The Salvation of Little Children

Bruce R. McConkie

Among all the glorious gospel verities given of God to his people there is scarcely a doctrine so sweet, so soul satisfying, and so soul sanctifying, as the one which proclaims—

Little children shall be saved. They are alive in Christ and shall have eternal life. For them the family unit will continue, and the fulness of exaltation is theirs. No blessing shall be withheld. They shall rise in immortal glory, grow to full maturity, and live forever in the highest heaven of the celestial kingdom—all through the merits and mercy and grace of the Holy Messiah, all because of the atoning sacrifice of Him who died that we might live.

One of the great benefits of the recent addition to the Doctrine and Covenants of Joseph Smith's Vision of the Celestial Kingdom (section 137) is the opportunity it affords to study anew the doctrine relative to the salvation of children. There are many valid questions which confront us in this field which are deserving of sound scriptural answers.

Two scenes showing the infinite love, tenderness, and compassion of the Lord Jesus set the stage for our consideration of the various matters involved in the salvation of children.

The first scene is set in "the coasts of Judea beyond Jordan." Great multitudes are before him; the Pharisees are querulous, seeking to entrap; he has just preached about marriage and divorce and the family unit. "Then were

From *Ensign*, April 1977, pp. 3-7.

there brought unto him little children," Matthew records, "that he should put his hands on them and pray. And the disciples rebuked them, saying, There is no need, for *Jesus hath said, Such shall be saved.*

"But Jesus said, Suffer little children to come unto me, and forbid them not, *for of such is the kingdom of heaven.*

"And he laid hands on them, and departed thence." (Joseph Smith Translation, Matthew 19:13-15. Italics added.)

The second scene is portrayed on the American continent. That same Jesus, the Compassionate One, risen and glorified, is ministering among his Nephite kinsmen. He has just prayed as none other had ever done before. "No tongue can speak, neither can there be written by any man, neither can the hearts of men conceive so great and marvelous things as we both saw and heard Jesus speak," the Nephite historian records. (3 Nephi 17:17.)

Then Jesus wept, and said: "Behold your little ones. . . .

"And they saw the heavens open, and they saw angels descending out of heaven as it were in the midst of fire; and they came down and encircled those little ones about, and they were encircled about with fire; and the angels did minister unto them." (3 Nephi 17:23-24.)

Jesus loves and blesses children. They are the companions of angels. They shall be saved. Of such is the kingdom of heaven.

Now let us record brief answers to the more commonly asked questions about the salvation of children.

Speaking of the Prophet's statement that all children are saved in the celestial kingdom, President Joseph Fielding Smith said: "This would mean the children of every race. All the spirits that come to this world come from the presence of God and, therefore, must have been in his kingdom. . . . Every spirit of man was innocent in the beginning; and all who rebelled were cast out; therefore, all who remained are entitled to the blessings of the gospel." (*Doctrines of Salvation*, Bookcraft, 1955, 2:55.)

How and why are they saved?

They are saved through the atonement and because

they are free from sin. They come from God in purity; no sin or taint attaches to them in this life; and they return in purity to their Maker. Accountable persons must become pure through repentance and baptism and obedience. Those who are not accountable for sins never fall spiritually and need not be redeemed from a spiritual fall which they never experienced. Hence the expression that little children are alive in Christ. "Little children are redeemed from the foundation of the world through mine Only Begotten," the Lord says. (D&C 29:46.)

Will they have eternal life?

Eternal life is life in the highest heaven of the celestial world; it is exaltation; it is the name of the kind of life God lives. It consists of a continuation of the family unit in eternity. We have quoted scriptures saying that children will be saved in the celestial kingdom, but now face the further query as to whether this includes the greatest of all the gifts of God—the gift of eternal life. And in the providences of Him who is infinitely wise, the answer is in the affirmative. Salvation means eternal life; the two terms are synonymous; they mean exactly the same thing. Joseph Smith said, "Salvation consists in the glory, authority, majesty, power and dominion which Jehovah possesses and in nothing else." (*Lectures on Faith*, pp. 63-67.) We have come to speak of this salvation as exaltation—which it is—but all of the scriptures in all of the standard works call it salvation. I know of only three passages in all our scriptures which use salvation to mean something other and less than exaltation.

Are children conceived in sin?

Since there is no such thing as original sin, as that expression is used in modern Christendom, it follows that children are not conceived in sin. They do not come into the world with any taint of impurity whatever. When our scriptures say that "children are conceived in sin," they are using words in an entirely different way than when the same language is recited in the creeds of the world. The scriptural meaning is that they are born into a world of sin so that "when they begin to grow up, sin conceiveth in their hearts, and they taste the bitter, that they may know to prize the good." (Moses 6:55.)

What about infant baptism?

Few false doctrines have ever deserved and received such a vigorous and forceful denunciation as that heaped upon infant baptism by the prophet Mormon. When that inspired author inquired of the Lord concerning the baptism of little children, he was told: "Listen to the words of Christ, your Redeemer, your Lord and your God. Behold, I came into the world not to call the righteous but sinners to repentance; the whole need no physician, but they that are sick; wherefore, little children are whole, for they are not capable of committing sin; wherefore the curse of Adam is taken from them in me, that it hath no power over them."

Thereupon Mormon, speaking by the power of the Holy Ghost, taught that "it is solemn mockery" to baptize little children; that they "are alive in Christ from the foundation of the world"; that it is awful wickedness to deny the pure mercies of Christ to them; that such a belief sets at naught the power of Christ's redemption; that those who believe such a false concept are "in the bonds of iniquity" and if cut off while in the thought shall be thrust down to hell; and that those who humble themselves and repent and are baptized shall "be saved with their little children." (Moroni 8:8-25.)

Are all little children saved automatically in the celestial kingdom?

To this question the answer is a thunderous *yes*, with echoes and re-echoes from one end of heaven to the other. Jesus taught it to his disciples. Mormon said it over and over again. Many of the prophets have spoken about it, and it is implicit in the whole plan of salvation. If it were not so the redemption would not be infinite in its application. And so, as we would expect, Joseph Smith's Vision of the Celestial Kingdom contains this statement: "And I also beheld that all children who die before they arrive at the years of accountability are saved in the celestial kingdom of heaven." (D&C 138:10.)

It is sometimes asked if this applies to children of all races, and of course the answer is that when the revelation says all children it means all children. There is no restriction as to race, kindred, or tongue. Little children are little children and they are all alive in Christ, and all are saved by him, through and because of the atonement.

What is a child and who are children?

A child is an adult spirit in a newly born body, a body capable of growing and maturing according to the providences of Him whose spirit children we all are. Children are the sons and daughters of God. They lived and dwelt with him for ages and eons before their mortal birth. They are adults before birth; they are adults at death. Christ himself, the Firstborn of the Father, rose to a state of glory and exaltation before he was ever suckled at Mary's breast.

What is mortal birth?

It is the process by which mature, sentient, intelligent beings pass from preexistence into a mortal sphere. It is the process by which we bring from premortality to mortality the traits and talents acquired and developed in our long years of spirit existence. It is the process by which a mortal body is created from the dust of the earth to house an eternal spirit offspring of the Father of us all. Mortality is fully upon us when we first breathe the breath of life.

Why are we born upon this earth?

We come here to gain bodies, bodies of flesh and blood, bodies which—following the natural death—we will receive back again in immortality. Those of us who arrive at the years of accountability are here to develop and to be tried and tested, to see if we can so live as to regain the state of innocence and purity which we enjoyed as children, and thereby be qualified to go where God and Christ are.

What is original sin?

This is the false doctrine that the sin of Adam passes upon all men and that, therefore, all men—infants included—must be baptized to be saved. It is, however, a fundamental principle of true religion "that men will be punished for their own sins, and not for Adam's transgression." (Article of Faith 2.)

Are children tainted with original sin?

Absolutely not. There is no such thing as original sin as such is defined in the creeds of Christendom. Such a concept denies the efficacy of the atonement. Our revelation says: "Every spirit of man was innocent in the beginning"—meaning that spirits started out in a state of purity and innocence in preexistence—"and God having redeemed man from the fall, men became again, in their infant state, innocent before God" (D&C 93:38)—meaning that all children start out their mortal probation in purity and innocence because of the atonement. Our revelations also say, "The Son of God hath atoned for original guilt, wherein the sins of the parents cannot be answered upon the heads of the children, for they are whole from the foundation of the world." (Moses 6:54.)

Abinadi said, "Little children also have eternal life." (Mosiah 15:25.) Joseph Smith taught, "Children will be enthroned in the presence of God and the Lamb; . . . they will there enjoy the fulness of that light, glory, and intelligence, which is prepared in the celestial kingdom." (*Teachings of the Prophet Joseph Smith,* p. 200.) President Joseph Fielding Smith spoke very expressly on this point: "The Lord will grant unto these children the privilege of all the sealing blessings which pertain to the exaltation. We were all mature spirits before we were born, and the bodies of little children will grow after the resurrection to the full stature of the spirit, and all the blessings will be theirs through their obedience, the same as if they had lived to maturity and received them on the earth. The Lord is just and will not deprive any person of a blessing, simply because he dies before that blessing can be received. It would be manifestly unfair to deprive a little child of the privilege of receiving all the blessings of exaltation in the world to come simply because it died in infancy. . . . Children who die in childhood will not be deprived of any blessing. When they grow, after the resurrection, to the full maturity of the spirit, they will be entitled to all the blessings which they would have been entitled to had they been privileged to tarry here and receive them." (*Doctrines of Salvation* 2:54.)

Will children be married and live in the family unit?

Certainly. There can be no question about this. If they gain salvation, which is eternal life, which is exaltation, it means that they are married and live in the family unit. President Joseph Fielding Smith has so stated in plain words, and it is something that must necessarily be so. (See *Doctrines of Salvation* 2:49-57.)

Why do some children die and others live? Are those who die better off than those who remain in mortality?

We may rest assured that all things are controlled and governed by Him whose spirit children we are. He knows the end from the beginning, and he provides for each of us the testings and trials which he knows we need. President Joseph Fielding Smith once told me that we must assume that the Lord knows and arranges beforehand who shall be taken in infancy and who shall remain on earth to undergo whatever tests are needed in their cases. This accords with Joseph Smith's statement: "The Lord takes many away, even in infancy, that they may escape the envy of man, and the sorrows and evils of this present world; they were too pure, too lovely, to live on earth." (*Teachings*, pp. 196-97.) It is implicit in the whole scheme of things that those of us who have arrived at the years of accountability need the tests and trials to which we are subject and that our problem is to overcome the world and attain that spotless and pure state which little children already possess.

*How much do children know before their mortal birth
about God and the plan of salvation?*

Every person born into the world comes from the
presence of God. We all saw him in that eternal world. We
heard his voice. He taught us his laws. We learned about
Christ and chose to follow him when he was chosen to be
our Savior and Redeemer. We understood and knew the
gospel plan and shouted for joy at the privilege of getting
our mortal bodies as part of that great plan of salvation.
Returning pure and spotless to their Maker, children—who
in reality are adults—will again have that gospel
knowledge which once was theirs.

Will children ever be tested?

Absolutely not! Any idea that they will be tested in
paradise or during the millennium or after the millennium
is pure fantasy. Why would a resurrected being, who has already come forth from the grave with a celestial body and
whose salvation is guaranteed, be tested? Would the Lord
test someone who cannot fail the test and whose exaltation
is guaranteed? For that matter, all those billions of people
who will be born during the millennium, when Satan is
bound, "shall grow up without sin unto salvation" (D&C
45:58) and therefore will not be tested. "Satan cannot
tempt little children in this life, nor in the spirit world, nor
after their resurrection. Little children who die before
reaching the years of accountability will not be tempted."
(*Doctrines of Salvation* 2:56-57.) Such is the emphatic language of President Joseph Fielding Smith.

What is the age of accountability?

Accountability does not burst full-bloom upon a child
at any given moment in his life. Children become accountable gradually, over a number of years. Becoming accountable is a process, not a goal to be attained when a specified
number of years, days, and hours have elapsed. In our
revelation the Lord says, "They cannot sin, for power is not
given unto Satan to tempt little children, until they begin

to become accountable before me." (D&C 29:47.) There comes a time, however, when accountability is real and actual and sin is attributed in the lives of those who develop normally. It is eight years of age, the age of baptism. (D&C 68:27.)

This principle of accountability has been twisted and perverted and even lost at various times. It was at the root of Mormon's inquiry to the Lord about infant baptism. (See Moroni 8.) One of our most instructive passages on the point contains the words spoken by the Lord to Abraham. "My people have gone astray from my precepts, and have not kept mine ordinances, which I gave unto their fathers," the Lord said.

"And they have not observed mine anointing, and the burial, or baptism wherewith I commanded them;

"But have turned from the commandment, and taken unto themselves the washing of children, and the blood of sprinkling." (*JST* Genesis 17:4-6.)

Infant baptism was practiced by some even in those early days. The reason? Men no longer understood the atonement. For, as the record continues, those ancient peoples "said that the blood of the righteous Abel was shed for sins; and have not known wherein they are accountable before me." (*JST* Genesis 17:7.)

Then the Lord made this promise to Abraham: "I will establish a covenant of circumcision with thee, and it shall be my covenent between me and thee, and thy seed after thee, in their generations; that thou mayest know for ever that children are not accountable before me until they are eight years old." (*JST* Genesis 17:11.)

What about the mentally deficient?

It is with them as it is with little children. They never arrive at the years of accountability and are considered as though they were little children. If because of some physical deficiency, or for some other reason unknown to us, they never mature in the spiritual and moral sense, then they never become accountable for sins. They need no baptism; they are alive in Christ; and they will receive, inherit, and possess in eternity on the same basis as do all children.

After revealing that little children are redeemed from the foundation of the world through the atoning sacrifice of Him who died to save us all, and after specifying that Satan has no power to tempt little children until they begin to become accountable, the Lord applied the same principles to those who are mentally deficient: "And, again, I say unto you, that whoso having knowledge, have I not commanded to repent? And he that hath no understanding, it remaineth in me to do according as it is written." (D&C 29:49-50.)

When and with what stature will children be resurrected?

Because they will receive a celestial inheritance, they will come forth in the first resurrection. President Joseph F. Smith said: "Joseph Smith taught the doctrine that the infant child that was laid away in death would come up in the resurrection as a child; and, pointing to the mother of a lifeless child, he said to her: 'You will have the joy, the pleasure, and satisfaction of nurturing this child, after its resurrection, until it reaches the full stature of its spirit.' There is restitution, there is growth, there is development, after the resurrection from death. I love this truth. It speaks volumes of happiness, of joy and gratitude to my soul. Thank the Lord he has revealed these principles to us." (*Gospel Doctrine*, pp. 455-56.)

What is our responsibility to our children?

"Lo, children are an heritage of the Lord: and the fruit of the womb is his reward." (Psalm 127:3.) Our children are our Father's children. He has entrusted them to us for a time and a season. Our appointment is to bring them up in light and truth so they will qualify to return to his Eternal Presence.

Parents in Zion have an especial responsibility for the care and well-being of the souls entrusted to them. King Benjamin summarized it in these words: "Ye will not suffer your children that they go hungry, or naked; neither will ye suffer that they transgress the laws of God, and fight and quarrel one with another, and serve the devil, who is the master of sin, or who is the evil spirit which hath been spoken of by our fathers, he being an enemy to all righteousness.

"But ye will teach them to walk in the ways of truth and soberness; ye will teach them to love one another, and to serve one another." (Mosiah 4:14-15. See also D&C 68:25-28.)

What, then, of this glorious doctrine concerning the salvation of children?

Truly it is one of the sweetest and most soul-satisfying doctrines of the gospel! It is also one of the great evidences of the divine mission of the Prophet Joseph Smith. In his day the fiery evangelists of Christendom were thundering from their pulpits that the road to hell is paved with the skulls of infants not a span long because careless parents had neglected to have their offspring baptized. Joseph Smith's statements, as recorded in the Book of Mormon and latter-day revelation, came as a refreshing breeze of pure truth: *little children shall be saved.* Thanks be to God for the revelations of his mind where these innocent and pure souls are concerned!

What After Death?

LeGrand Richards

I thought today that I would like to direct what I have to say to those parents who have lost children in death before they reached maturity and could enter into the covenant of marriage and have their own children here upon this earth. I reckon that there aren't many families who haven't had that experience.

I think of the thousands of our boys who have lost their lives on the battlefields of their various countries. I think of our boys who have died in the mission field. While I was president of the Netherlands Mission, I held one of those wonderful missionaries in my arms as he passed on to eternal glory.

I think of the many wonderful, faithful women who never have an opportunity to marry here in mortality because they are not willing to throw their lives away on men who are not worthy to take them to the celestial kingdom. Many of them have filled missions and work diligently for the upbuilding of our Father's kingdom, for the raising of the youth of Zion, and they are wonderful.

I would like to use my own family as an illustration of what I have in mind. Mother and I were filling a mission together over in Holland when we had a little girl born to us, and after we had been home a few years she passed away. When she was born, my wife has told me over and over again that she felt she saw an angel bring that spirit to

Address delivered at the 144th Semiannual General Conference of the Church, October 1974. Published in *Ensign*, November 1974, pp. 52-54.

her. And yet she is gone. Then I think of her four sisters. You voted here today to sustain one of them as a counselor in the general presidency of the Relief Society. Her other three sisters are just as noble and wonderful, although their talents may be just a little different.

When I think of this little one that we laid away when she was three-and-a-half years old, I thank God I have the faith to believe that God reigns in the heavens above and in the earth beneath and that this little one will ultimately enter into her glory and be equal to any of her four sisters who have tarried here upon this earth and raised their families. I thank God for the statement of the apostle Paul when he said that "If in this life only we have hope in Christ, we are of all men most miserable." (1 Corinthians 15:19.) In this brief period of mortality, it would not be possible for God to accomplish for all of his children all that he has in mind for them, the ones that are true and faithful.

I think of the statement of Moses as recorded in the Pearl of Great Price: "For behold, this is my work and my glory—to bring to pass the immortality and eternal life of man." (Moses 1:39.) I wonder sometimes if we ever stop to analyze that statement. I think we can understand what "to bring to pass immortality" is, that we will never die after we come forth in the resurrection, as President Romney pointed out this morning. But about eternal life? As I interpret this, I find in it the feeling that all that God has ultimately planned for his children who are faithful and true shall come to them in his own due time.

We read in the Book of Mormon that we are not all born at the same time (and that doesn't matter) and that we don't all die at the same time. (See Alma 40:8.) I think of the words of Abraham when he saw the placing of the spirits here upon this earth, that the Lord would prove them to see if they would do all things whatsoever he had commanded them. Then he adds: "And they who keep their first estate shall be added upon." (Abraham 3:26.) That was in the spirit life before we came to mortality. "They who keep their second estate shall have glory added upon their heads for ever and ever." (Abraham 3:26.) This little girl of ours kept her second estate as far as she could at her age.

Then I think of the statement of the Lord to the Prophet Joseph Smith when he said: "The works, and the designs, and the purposes of God cannot be frustrated, neither can they come to naught." (D&C 3:1.) In other words, no one can stand in the way of God achieving what he has decreed for his children. Then a further statement in the Doctrine and Covenants where the Lord said: "His purposes fail not, neither are there any who can stay his hand. From eternity to eternity he is the same." (D&C 76:3-4.)

Then there are the words of the Lord to the prophet Nephi when he said: "For my work is not yet finished; neither shall it be until the end of man, neither from that time henceforth and forever." (2 Nephi 29:9.) Now that should enable us to comprehend and realize that there will never be a time when God will cease to do his work to bring to pass, as we read in the Pearl of Great Price, the glory that will be added upon their heads forever and ever.

Coming back to our family, we had four daughters before we got a boy and he grew into beautiful young manhood; we lost him in an accident down at the beach in California while I was the president of the stake there. He was just turning sixteen and he stood as tall as his father, and to think now of his own brothers who are here: they have their families, and one of them has just been serving as one of the Regional Representatives of the Twelve. I can't believe that boy will come out any less exalted in the eternities that are to come than his brothers who have lived here in mortality. When he died, the principle of the high school came to our home (and he was not a member of the Church) and told Sister Richards that our son was the best boy he had ever had in his school, and we felt that, too, as he grew into manhood.

Then I think of our little granddaughter who died at the same age; her father and mother are here today and her brothers and sisters. After just a few days of sickness, she passed away at the age of sixteen, a beautiful little woman. To think that God's plan would not ultimately bring to her everything our other children received who tarried here in mortality would lessen my appreciation of my Father in heaven and the perfectness of his plan.

I think of the parable Jesus gave when he said: "For which of you, intending to build a tower, sitteth not down first, and counteth the cost, whether he have sufficient to finish it? Lest haply, after he hath laid the foundation, and is not able to finish it, all that behold it begin to mock him." (Luke 14:28-29.)

If God started to bring to pass the immortality and eternal life of man and did not provide an opportunity to complete the program, he would be like the builder who starts to build and then is not able to finish.

Coming back, then, to the family, I think of my wife's sister who died here a short time ago. She filled a mission for the Church; she worked in the auxiliaries and she was a noble character. But she never married, and I can't believe that the Lord's plan is imperfect, that she will not ultimately enjoy all that her sister (my wife) with our wonderful family has enjoyed. "His purposes fail not, neither are there any who can stay his hand." (D&C 76:3.)

So I thank God for the thousand years of the millennial reign. My, what a lot of work needs to be done during that period!

I can't take time to tell you much about that, but I think of the words of Isaiah. He had a glimpse of it. He saw the day when we would have a new heaven and a new earth, when the wolf and the lion would lie down together, and the lion would eat straw like the ox. His people should build houses and inhabit them, and should plant vineyards and eat the fruit thereof. They should not build and another inhabit. They should not plant and another eat, for every man would enjoy the work of his own hands. (See Isaiah 65:17-25 and 11:6-9.) Then he adds: "For they are the seed of the blessed of the Lord, and their offspring with them." (Isaiah 65:23.) That sounds like a continuation of the family, doesn't it?

Then I thank God for the statement of the apostle Paul when he said: "Neither is the man without the woman, neither the woman without the man, in the Lord." (1 Corinthians 11:11.) That being true, the Lord must have a plan so that these children can ultimately enjoy that great blessing.

I will now read you a statement from the Lord regarding this millennial reign. He said:

"And there shall be no sorrow because there shall be no death.

"In that day an infant shall not die until he is old; and his life shall be as the age of a tree;

"And when he dies he shall not sleep, that is to say in the earth, but shall be changed in the twinkling of an eye, and shall be caught up, and his rest shall be glorious." (D&C 101:29-31.)

So he is to live to the age of a tree, and then he is to be changed in the twinkling of an eye.

I want to read you one more statement of the Lord to the Prophet Joseph:

"And the earth shall be given unto them for an inheritance; and they shall multiply and wax strong, (*and they can't multiply unless they have that relationship of husband and wife*) and their children shall grow up without sin unto salvation.

"For the Lord shall be in their midst, and his glory shall be upon them, and he will be their king and their lawgiver." (D&C 45:58-59.)

Then I think of the revelation concerning those who will inherit the celestial kingdom, and the Lord said: ". . . which glory shall be a fulness and a continuation of the seeds forever and ever." (D&C 132:19.)

And so I expect some day to see the bride that my son has selected over there in the spirit world. If he can find one as noble as his little niece I have mentioned (my granddaughter), just think what a glorious day that will be. In order to properly understand this, I would like to read a couple of statements: one from President Brigham Young about what will happen during the Millennium, and one from President Wilford Woodruff.

President Young said: "To accomplish this work there will have to be not only one temple, but thousands of them, and thousands and tens of thousands of men and women will go into those temples and officiate for people who have lived as far back as the Lord shall reveal." (*Journal of Discourses* 3:372.) Just think—if there are going to be thousands of temples and tens of thousands of people going to them, it will give you a little idea of what the Lord has in store for these spirits who have to have their temple work done.

Then the Prophet Wilford Woodruff said: "When the Savior comes, a thousand years will be devoted to this work of redemption and temples will appear all over this land of Joseph—North and South America—and also in Europe and elsewhere." (JD 19:230.)

I close my remarks today with my faith that the Lord knows what he is doing and he has prepared a plan so that those who have gone before will not suffer. I therefore conclude with the words of the apostle Paul, who was caught up into the third heaven and paradise of God, and he saw things he was not permitted to write. But he did say: "Eye hath not seen, nor ear heard, neither have entered into the heart of man, the things which God hath prepared for them that love him." (1 Corinthians 2:9.) That is my faith in my God, and I leave you my blessing in the name of the Lord, Jesus Christ. Amen.

The Death of a Child: A Prophet's Perspective

Brent A. Barlow

When a couple marry and begin to have children, they usually anticipate many joyful and fulfilling experiences as a family. There are traditional festive celebrations, such as Thanksgiving and Christmas, birthdays, vacations and visits to relatives, and many other pleasant occasions that are often shared and enjoyed by families. For Latter-day Saints there are also weekly family home evenings, participation in Church activities and programs, and family prayers, all of which tend to solidify and promote family unity.

With the many pleasant experiences in family life, however, there are often also times of stress. Many of these situations are external or arise outside the family unit, such as unemployment of the providing parent, or extended absence of a parent because of military service or other obligations away from home. Other kinds of family stress include severe illness of a family member, particularly if it requires hospitalization, alcoholism, drug addiction, delinquency, desertion, divorce, imprisonment, suicide, institutionalization for mental illness, and the death of a child, spouse, or parent.

Death is a unique form of family crisis, one that all families will experience. Though we may try to deny death, we know we will eventually encounter it, often beginning with the loss of a grandparent or an elderly relative. As we grow older, we also realize that we will lose both our parents through death. After marriage, it is understood that one spouse will sustain the loss of the other through the process of dying. Gradually we begin to accept the fact that death is an inevitable part of living.

Another reality of death is that the vast majority of people die after living several decades, usually after age sixty, and have usually lived productive, fulfilling lives. We generally have an opportunity to prepare gradually for the death of an aging loved one as we begin to witness a decline in health or notice other events related to the aging process.

Though the death of any member of the family produces stress, the death of a younger family member, a child, is particularly difficult to face. "Why our child?" parents may ask. Few events are more emotionally painful for a husband and wife to experience than losing a child through death.

Perhaps some perspective can be placed on this question by examining the life and teachings of the Prophet Joseph Smith. He had to face this question in his own life several times, and was called upon to comfort and reassure other parents who lost children through death.

On March 20, 1842, at a service for the deceased child of Windsor P. Lyon, the Prophet commented, ". . . in my leisure moments I have meditated upon the subject, and asked the question, why it is that infants, innocent children, are taken away from us, especially those that seem to be the most intelligent and interesting." (*History of the Church* 4:553.) His concern with the death of children was of more than fleeting interest. Just seven months earlier, on August 15, 1841, he had recorded in his journal: "Sunday, 15.—My infant son, Don Carlos, died, aged 14 months, 2 days." (HC 4:402.) This was, indeed, a tragic event in the life of the Prophet and his wife Emma. It was not, however, the first time—nor would it be the last time—they would experience the death of a child. During their marriage nine children were born to them, and they also adopted two others. Six of these eleven children died at birth or during infancy.

We sometimes fail to remember that in addition to being the prophet who ushered in the dispensation of the fulness of times, Joseph Smith was also a husband and father.

As such, he would have had the same tender feelings toward his wife and children as would any other man.

The reality of being separated from his family was difficult for Joseph to bear. While imprisoned in Missouri he once wrote to Emma: "O, God grant that I may have the privilege of seeing once more my lovely family, in the enjoyment of the sweets of liberty and social life; to press them to my bosom and kiss their lovely cheeks would fill my heart with unspeakable gratitude. Tell the children that I am alive and trust that I shall come and see them before long. Comfort their hearts all you can, and try to be comforted yourself, all you can." (As quoted in E. Cecil McGavin, *The Family of Joseph Smith*, Bookcraft, 1963, p. 159.)

One can hardly imagine, therefore, the emotional heartaches of Joseph and Emma when their first four children died at birth or soon thereafter. Alva, their first son, was born June 15, 1828, at Harmony, Pennsylvania, and lived but a few minutes. Joseph's mother, Lucy Mack Smith, wrote of this incident: "Shortly after Mr. [Martin] Harris left, Joseph's wife became the mother of a son, which, however, remained with her but a short time before it was snatched from her arms by the hand of death. And the mother seemed, for some time, more like sinking with her infant into the mansion of the dead, than remaining with her husband among the living. Her situation was such for two weeks, that Joseph slept not an hour in undisturbed quiet." (*History of Joseph Smith by His Mother*, Bookcraft, 1958, p. 125.)

Three years after they moved to Ohio, Emma gave birth to twins, a boy, Thaddeus, and a girl, Louisa, on April 30, 1831. Both lived only two or three hours. On the same day the Smith twins died, another Latter-day Saint woman, a Sister Murdock, also gave birth to twins in nearby Orange, Ohio. She died shortly after the birth, but the twins survived. Nine days later the father, John Murdock, took the twins to the bereaved Joseph and Emma and asked them to adopt the infants. The Smiths received them gladly and did adopt them. They named the boy Joseph Smith

Murdock, and the girl, Julia. It was indeed a rare but timely gift for the Prophet and his wife.

Little did the Smiths realize that their new son, Joseph, would die before his first birthday. On March 24, 1832, Joseph and Emma were living in Hiram, Ohio. That evening they were attending to the twins, who had measles, and Emma had retired with Julia, while Joseph was tending their son, who was very ill. Suddenly vicious mobbers broke into the home and dragged the Prophet to a nearby field, where they tarred and feathered him. The sick infant, Joseph Smith Murdock, barely eleven months old, was left in the home exposed to the inclement weather, caught a severe cold, and died soon after.

Fortunately, Joseph and Emma did have children who lived. The adopted Julia lived to be their oldest child, and two other children, sons, were born while the family was living in Ohio. Joseph Smith III was born November 6, 1832, and Frederick Granger Williams Smith was born on June 20, 1836. After the Saints moved to Missouri, Emma gave birth to Alexander Hale Smith on June 2, 1838. Shortly after they settled in Nauvoo, Illinois, Don Carlos Smith was born on June 13, 1840; he died fourteen months later, on August 15, 1841. Another infant son, unnamed, died at birth on December 26, 1842, one day after Christmas and three days after the Prophet's birthday. David Hyrum Smith, whom the Prophet never saw, was born in Nauvoo on November 27, 1844, just five months after his father's martyrdom. Having lost six children by death, it is little wonder that Joseph Smith often contemplated why infants, innocent children, are taken away from us.

Perhaps it was because of his frequent experiences with the deaths of his own children that the Prophet was able to give us important insights into the status of children after death, parent-child relationships after death, and some understanding of why infants die. As Latter-day Saints, we should be grateful for a prophet's perspective to help us understand, in part, this painful and often difficult event so many parents have experienced or may yet encounter.

Status of Children after Death

Undoubtedly many parents of deceased children wonder about the condition of their children after death and ask what, if any, are the possibilities of salvation. While there are many beliefs on this subject among various religious denominations, Joseph Smith's teachings and revelations on the status of *all* children after death are both concise and consoling.

His first insights on the subject were probably gained while he was translating the Book of Mormon. In Mosiah we read Abinadi's statement that "little children also have eternal life." (Mosiah 15:25.) Mormon's great epistle to his son Moroni pertaining to the status of children and salvation teaches us that "little children are whole, for they are not capable of committing sin," and "little children are alive in Christ, even from the foundation of the world; if not so, God is a partial God, and also a changeable God, and a respecter to persons; for how many little children have died without baptism!" (Moroni 8:8, 12.) Even though Joseph Smith was not directly responsible for these particular teachings, he was instrumental in bringing about these important but lost truths when he translated and published the Book of Mormon.

On September 26, 1830, in Fayette, New York, just seven months before the deaths of Thaddeus and Louisa, the Lord revealed to the Prophet, ". . . behold, I say unto you, that little children are redeemed from the foundation of the world through mine Only Begotten." (D&C 29:46.) In January 1832, at Hiram, Ohio, just two months before the death of Joseph Smith Murdock, the Prophet learned that "little children are holy, being sanctified through the atonement of Jesus Christ." (D&C 74:7.)

Four years later, on January 21, 1832, he received the following revelation while in the Kirtland Temple: "All who have died without a knowledge of this gospel, who would have received it if they had been permitted to tarry, shall be heirs of the celestial kingdom of God; Also all that shall die henceforth without a knowledge of it, who would have received it with all their hearts, shall be heirs of that kingdom; For I, the Lord, will judge all men according to their works, according to the desire of their hearts." Then the Prophet added: "And I also beheld that all children who die before they arrive at the years of accountability are saved in the celestial kingdom of heaven." (D&C 137:7-10.)

On March 20, 1842, just seven months after the death of their infant son Don Carlos, the Prophet declared at the memorial service of another deceased child: "The doctrine of baptizing children, or sprinkling them, or they must welter in hell, is a doctrine not true, not supported in Holy Writ, and is not consistent with the character of God. All children are redeemed by the blood of Jesus Christ, and the moment that children leave this world, they are taken to the bosom of Abraham. The only difference between the old and young dying is, one lives longer in heaven and eternal light and glory than the other, and is freed a little sooner from this miserable, wicked world. Notwithstanding all this glory, we for a moment lose sight of it, and mourn the loss, but we do not mourn as those without hope." (HC 4:554.)

By way of summary, one of the most comforting truths ever uttered by the Prophet is found in the succinct statement: "all children who die before they arrive at the years of accountability are saved in the celestial kingdom of heaven."

Parent-Child Relationships after Death

Another consoling and unique aspect of Latter-day Saint theology came from Joseph Smith's teachings about the possibility of a parent-and-child relationship after death. In a meeting in the Nauvoo Temple on Sunday, April 16, 1843, just four months after the death of their newborn son, the Prophet read a letter from Parley P. Pratt informing the Saints of the death of a prominent missionary, Lorenzo Dow Barnes, who died en route to a foreign mission. After reading the letter, the Prophet spoke for two hours, trying to console the grieving Saints, many of whom had recently lost loved ones through death. He promised them, "All your losses will be made up to you in the resurrection, provided you continue faithful. By the vision of the Almighty I have seen it." (HC 5:362.)

On the condition that they prove to be faithful, the Saints were given the assurance that any loss of a loved one sustained during mortality would be made up to them after the resurrection. For the Prophet, the reuniting of family members after death was more than just a pleasant thought, for he actually saw it in vision and described it:

"Would you think it strange if I relate what I have seen in vision in relation to this interesting theme? Those who have died in Jesus Christ may expect to enter into all that fruition of joy when they come forth, which they possessed or anticipated here.

"So plain was the vision, that I actually saw men, before they had ascended from the tomb, as though they were getting up slowly. They took each other by the hand and said to each other, 'My father, my son, my mother, my daughter, my brother, my sister.' And when the voice calls for the dead to arise, suppose I am laid by the side of my father, what would be the first joy of my heart? To meet my father, my mother, my brother, my sister; and when they are by my side, I embrace them and they me." (HC 5:361-62.)

On the conditions specified, the joyful reuniting of family members during the resurrection was apparently only the commencement of the family or parent-child relationship, "provided you continue faithful."

It was evidently at the funeral service of his niece Sophronia that Joseph Smith first taught this doctrine. The child died in October 1843, and her father, Don Carlos Smith, had died two years earlier on August 7, 1841, at the age of twenty-five. At the child's funeral service the Prophet pointed to Agnes Smith, the grieving mother, and said, "You will have the joy, the pleasure, and satisfaction of nurturing this child, after its resurrection, until it reaches the full stature of its spirit." (As quoted in Joseph F. Smith, *Gospel Doctrine*, 1928 ed., p. 575.)

President Joseph F. Smith, who was a nephew of the Prophet and later the sixth president of the Church, wrote: "I met with my aunt, the wife of my uncle, Don Carlos

Smith, who was the mother of that little girl that Joseph Smith, the Prophet, was speaking about when he told the mother that she should have the joy, the pleasure and satisfaction of rearing the child, after the resurrection, until it reached the full stature of its spirit; *and that it would be a far greater joy than she could possibly have in mortality, because she would be free from the sorrow and fear and disabilities of mortal life, and she would know more than she could know in this life.* I met that widow, the mother of that child, and she told me this circumstance and bore testimony to me that this was what the Prophet Joseph Smith said when he was speaking at the funeral of her little girl." (Ibid. Italics added.)

President Joseph F. Smith also reported a conversation with his brother-in-law, Lorin Walker, who mentioned he was present at the funeral of Sophronia Smith. President Smith asked, "Lorin, what did the Prophet say?" According to President Smith, Lorin Walker repeated, "as nearly as he could remember, what the Prophet Joseph said in relation to little children. The body remains undeveloped in the grave, but the spirit returns to God who gave it. Afterwards, in the resurrection, the spirit and body will be reunited; the body will develop and grow to the full stature of the spirit; and the resurrected soul will go on to perfection." (Ibid., pp. 575-76.)

M. Isabella Horne recalled a conversation with the Prophet in Nauvoo in which "the subject of children in the resurrection was broached. I believe it was in Sister Leonora Cannon Taylor's house. She had just lost one of her children, and I had also lost one previously. The Prophet wanted to comfort us, and he told us that we should receive those children in the morning of the resurrection just as we laid them down, in purity and innocence, and we should nourish and care for them as their mothers. He said that children would be raised in the resurrection just as they were laid down, and that they would obtain all the intelligence necessary to occupy thrones, principalities and powers. The idea that I got from what he said was that the children would grow and develop in the Millennium, and that the mothers would have the pleasure of training and caring for them, which they had been deprived of in this life." (HC 4:556.)

Joseph Horne, Isabella's husband, added, "I heard the Prophet Joseph Smith say that mothers should receive their children just as they laid them down, and that they would have the privilege of doing for them what they could not do here, the Prophet remarked, 'How would you know them if you did not receive them as you laid them down?' I also got the idea that children would grow and develop after the resurrection, and that the mothers would care for them and train them." (HC 4:556-57.)

On Sunday, April 7, 1844, just two months before his own death, the Prophet delivered a sermon to about twenty thousand Saints gathered in Nauvoo for general conference. Part of his remarks pertained to family members who had died. He said:

"I have a father, brothers, children, and friends who have gone to a world of spirits. They are only absent for a moment. They are in the spirit, and we shall soon meet again. . . . A question may be asked—'Will mothers have their children in eternity?' Yes! Yes! Mothers, you shall have your children; for they shall have eternal life, for their debt is paid. There is no damnation awaiting them for they are in the spirit. But as the child dies, so shall it rise from the dead, and be for ever living in the learning of God. It will never grow [in the grave]; it will still be the child, in the same precise form [when it rises] as it appeared before it died out of its mother's arms, but possessing all the intelligence of a God." (HC 6:316.)

Not only did the Prophet assure the young Agnes Smith and other mothers of a continued relationship with their deceased children, but he also taught that it "would be a far greater joy" than they possibly could have had during mortality. Apparently other Saints who have lost a child during this life will have a similar opportunity for a joyous parentage after the resurrection, provided they heed the Prophet's counsel to "continue faithful." Perhaps we now better understand and appreciate Paul's comment to the Saints in Corinth when he wrote, "If in this life only we have hope in Christ, we are of all men [and women] most miserable." (1 Corinthians 15:19.)

Why Infants Die

The Prophet Joseph Smith probably struggled even harder to obtain an answer to his query, "why it is that infants, innocent children, are taken away from us." (HC 4:553.) A belief prevalent in many religious denominations at that time was that death resulted from spiritual transgression or was used by God as punishment for the survivors. Often the death of a child was considered as the latter by many parents who felt they had sinned in some way and were being punished. Such beliefs were apparently also being entertained by some of the Saints, for on September 29, 1839, Joseph Smith addressed the topic and said, ". . . it is an unhallowed principle to say that such and such have transgressed because they have been preyed upon by disease or death, for all flesh is subject to death; and the Savior has said, 'Judge not, lest ye be judged.' " (HC 4:11.) He further elaborated: ". . . it is a false idea that the Saints will escape all the judgments, whilst the wicked suffer; for all flesh is subject to suffer, and 'the righteous shall hardly escape;' . . . many of the righteous shall fall a prey to disease, to pestilence, etc., by reason of the weakness of the flesh, and yet be saved in the Kingdom of God." (HC 4:11.)

As to why infants or children die, the Prophet stated that it was not necessarily because of sin on the part of parents or a family member. He taught that all flesh, including infants and children, is subject to suffer and may "fall prey to disease, pestilence, etc.," including accidents. In essence, all mortals are subject to death, regardless of age. He also gave some additional insights as to why infants or children die. He declared:

"The strongest reasons that present themselves to my mind are these: This world is a very wicked world; and it is a proverb that the 'world grows weaker and wiser;' if that is the case, the world grows more wicked and corrupt. In the earlier ages of the world a righteous man, and a man of God and of intelligence, had a better chance to do good, to be believed and received than at the present day: but in these days such a man is much opposed and persecuted by most of the inhabitants of the earth, and he has much sorrow to pass through here. The Lord takes many away, even in infancy, that they may escape the envy of man, and the sorrows and evils of this present world; they were too pure, too lovely, to live on earth; therefore, if rightly considered, instead of mourning we have reason to rejoice as they are delivered from evil, and we shall soon have them again." (HC 4:553.)

Here, then, are some perspectives of the Prophet Joseph Smith on the death of children. For such, we thank thee, O God, for a prophet!

The Locust Tree Shall Bloom Again

Pauline L. Jensen

The locust tree meant many things. To Mama it was a reminder of her childhood home in the sleepy, gentle Southern town where she had played beneath the boughs of another locust tree, which, too, had spread its protective arms above the kitchen roof. When Mama had come to the prairies as a bride, the lonely stretches of the land, bereft of friendly trees, had filled her with a poignant loneliness.

Then, on one of her infrequent trips back to her old home, Mama had, on her return, brought a locust sapling. She had planted it within reach of the kitchen stoop, tended it with loving care, and it had returned that care by growing straight and strong, and lifting up its boughs as though to thwart the molten sun and bitter winds that blew across the prairies. And Mama, unaccustomed to this harsh, demanding land, felt, in the locust tree, a link between the old life and the new one.

To Papa, the tree was a source of comfort, for he could sit within its shade when he returned from work and see the prairie sights and hear the prairie sounds he loved. At noon it gave him cooling shelter. At night the wind that blew unceasingly was tempered by the boughs into a gentle breeze.

To the children, the tree meant a dedicated place of play. Here they had their swing and hammock, and here they built their cities in the sand, and made mud pies. And here their collie burrowed close against the house and watched them at their play. And every year a pair of robins

From *Relief Society Magazine*, vol. 48 (1961), pp. 242-43.

nested in the leafy branches of the tree and fretted at the children down below.

And still the locust tree had yet another meaning, a deeper one by far. For it was a harbinger of spring, both of the land and of the spirit. For with the blooming of the tree, the meadow larks were heard to sing, and fields of winter wheat began to green. And long before the blooming, Mama watched with eager eyes for signs of the tree's awakening. When it came, she would say with lilting voice, "Our Father is good. He has wrought another spring, and now the locust tree will bloom again."

Then one day in late winter, death stalked the small community, and Mama's firstborn son, young and handsome, was taken from her. Mama's heart was frozen, and her face wore a still and quiet look. She did not cry, but neither did she smile. She brushed aside the clumsy efforts Papa made to comfort her, and walked the days as though alone, uncaring.

That spring the locust tree bloomed gloriously, but Mama did not notice. The children gathered handfuls of the fragrant blossoms and brought them to her, but she only stared at them in silence. All through the summer the children brought her offerings; the newest kittens, which she stroked mechanically, but did not cuddle as had been her wont. And when, in fall, they gathered armloads of the prairie goldenrod, she only turned unseeing eyes upon it.

When winter settled down upon the land, Mama did not read aloud to the children the Bible stories that they loved. When they asked for them, she turned a bitter look upon them, and shook her head. And it was Papa, now, who heard the prayers at night, instead of Mama. Mama's face was set and cold, her thoughts remote, withdrawn.

Then spring once more cast its spell upon the land. There came an April evening of mauve and gold skies, and undulating green across the prairie floor. The children played beneath the tree, and Papa rested on the kitchen stoop. They all looked up in surprise as Mama stepped outside. In her hands she held the worn and much-used Bible she had brought with her as a bride. Her hands caressed it lovingly. Her eyes were red from weeping, and her face, though still, had a different look; a washed and tranquil look, just like the earth after a quick and cleansing storm.

She paused and looked around her, as if she saw all for the first time after a long absence. Papa stared at her, and in his eyes a light began to glow. He reached out for her hand, and took it tenderly. She smiled at him and took a deep breath of the fresh, clean air. Then she raised her face unto the locust tree and spoke in wondering tones, "Our Father is good! He has wrought another spring, and now the locust tree will bloom again."

Explaining Death
to the Latter-day Saint Child

Brent A. Barlow

President Joseph F. Smith made the following statement: "Children are sure to be brought into some ac-
quaintanceship with the incident of death, even during the
kindergarten period; and it would be a great relief to the
puzzled and perplexed conditions of their minds if some intelligent statements of the reason for death were made to
them." (*Juvenile Instructor*, June 1, 1905, p. 336.)

It is evident both from President Smith's statement and
daily observation of the Latter-day Saint child that the
child is constantly learning about death. Many children's
stories, at least in the original versions, have death themes,
such as "Snow White," "Little Red Riding Hood," and
"The Three Little Pigs." In addition, some children's songs
("Rock-a-Bye Baby") and rhymes ("Humpty Dumpty")
may be interpreted by children to refer to death. Contemporary Latter-day Saint children also differ from children of
previous generations in that many view a great deal of television, which is heavily imbued with death and death-
related incidents. One survey indicated that the average
child in the U.S. watches television six hours a day, seven
days a week, which is 50 percent more time than he spends
in school. Watching television is the second largest
activity in many children's lives, second only to sleep. On
any given day a child can view several deaths, which com-
pound into literally hundreds and even thousands by the
time adulthood is attained. Questions are now being raised
about the numerous synthetic, quick deaths children observe in movies or on television. Tonight's villain is killed,

only to appear next week on another program in another role, thereby giving the child the impression that death is a temporary, emotionless event.

President Smith also observed: "It is a principle widely accepted that it is not desirable to teach these little ones those things that are horrifying to childish nature. And what may be said of children is equally true in all stages of student life. But death is not an unmixed horror. With it are associated some of the profoundest and most important truths of human life. Although painful in the extreme to those who must suffer the departure of dear ones, death is one of the grandest blessings in divine economy; *and we think children should be taught something of its true meaning as early in life as possible.*" (Ibid. Italics added.)

Children have differing views of death at different ages. In general, few children under the age of three have much comprehension of death, other than being separated from the deceased person, and are primarily concerned about someone caring for their physical, and to some degree, emotional needs. When a child experiences the death of a loved one, he needs to be assured verbally and perhaps by touch that there are others who still love him and will care for him.

Between the ages of about three and six, most children begin to understand death as a separation, but it is often perceived to be temporary or reversible, as symbolized in the fairy tale by the prince kissing Snow White and awakening her from her "sleep." Children during these ages can "kill" each other while playing cops and robbers because of the temporary nature of death.

From the age of six to about eight or nine, the child begins to understand the significance of death for others and the permanence of death during mortality. It is at about the age of nine that most children begin to realize the reality of their own death.

Several books and articles have recently been written with suggestions for explaining death to children. The following general guidelines have been condensed and modified for use by Latter-day Saint parents:

1. Explain that all living things die. This can be easily

observed with plants, pets, or any living thing with which the child is acquainted.

2. Discuss death with children before it occurs to someone they love. Much of death education is ex post facto—after the event. It would be helpful for most children to discuss death not only when it occurs, but also at a time when they are not experiencing the loss of a loved one.

3. Explain the permanence of death as far as mortality is concerned. Although there have been several instances reported in Church history in which deceased parents of family members appeared as spirits to mortals, it would be questionable to teach children to anticipate such an event with any degree of certainty when they lose loved ones through death. Once someone dies, it is probable that we will not see that person again during this life.

4. Caution should be used in making analogies about death. Telling a child, for example, that "Grandpa is taking a long journey" may be confusing, since people who go on long journeys usually return. Also, the implication that "he is asleep" is questionable because sleeping people usually awaken.

5. It would be wise to examine carefully the reasons given for death. "She died because she was sick" may be an inadequate answer, since it may cause unrealistic fear of sickness. Not all sick people die. Saying that "he died because he went to the hospital" may cause undue fear of hospitals, because not all people who go to the hospital die. Another commonly used reason is that a person died because he or she was old. What is "old" to a child? Someone has suggested that it may be anyone fifteen years older than the child. A simple statement such as "Grandmother died because her body (or parts of it, such as heart or lungs) ceased to function" may prove to be an adequate response to a child's inquiry as to why grandmother died. Parents should be honest, brief, and matter-of-fact in explaining death to children.

6. One of the most difficult aspects of death education is the theological implications often suggested in death. While our Heavenly Father could have been directly or in-

directly involved in a death, and this belief may be consoling to the adult, it is often a difficult phenomenon for the child to understand. A son, for instance, may wonder why his father was "needed on the other side" when he might also have a great need for his father at that particular time. Extreme care should be exercised in this particular area of explaining death to a child.

7. Children, particularly after the age of six or seven, should be allowed, but not forced, to participate in the mourning and funeral processes. Children, as do others, need to work through their own grief and should be allowed, if they desire, to participate in the social or public ceremonies at the time of death. If a child at any age chooses not to participate in the funeral or public mourning, he should not be made to feel guilty or that he has "let the family down."

8. Parents should do all they possibly can to alleviate any guilt a child may experience at the time of death. Sometimes a child will feel responsible for the death of a loved one because he, the child, acted badly or did something inappropriate, and is therefore being punished. If these feelings are carried to an excess, the child may need professional help. If a death, such as that of a grandparent, is equally difficult for all family members, parents may find it helpful to have another adult, a neighbor or relative, to attend or be with the child during the early stages of bereavement or during the funeral, so the child will not feel ignored.

9. Parents should make time available to discuss death sometime after children have experienced the loss of a loved one or a beloved pet. By agreeing to discuss death again at another time, death education becomes an ongoing process and not an isolated event.

10. The initial discussions of death with young children should not include their own death or that of immediate family members. It would probably be more helpful at the beginning to have general discussions about death (a) as a normal process of life, (b) of all living things, and (c) of other people with whom the child is not so intimately or emotionally involved. Discussions of the child's death or

that of parents, brothers, or sisters would best follow at other appropriate times.

In addition to these suggestions, Latter-day Saints should give some additional explanations to their children on at least three other significant aspects of death:

1. Explain that all men, women, boys, and girls have a body that eventually dies and a spirit that never dies (or is immortal). It is absolutely essential that children understand this part of our existence as early as possible. Without such an explanation, it may be extremely confusing to a child to watch a deceased uncle being buried in the ground and then to be told "Uncle Roy is now in heaven."

2. Explain that there is a life after death. While it may be questionable to imply that the child will see a deceased loved one again during mortality, it is certainly advisable to convey to the child our belief of the reuniting of loved ones in a life hereafter.

3. Teach children the reality of the death and resurrection of Jesus Christ. President Joseph F. Smith stated: "No explanation of death to a child's mind can anywhere be found that is more simple and convincing than is the death of our Master, connected as it is and ever must be with His glorious resurrection. . . . We are born that we may put on mortality, that is, that we may clothe our spirits with a body. Such a blessing is the first step toward an immortal body, and the second step is death. Death lies along the road of eternal progress; and though hard to bear, no one who believes in the Gospel of Jesus Christ, and especially in the resurrection, would have otherwise. Children should be taught early in life that death is really a necessity as well as a blessing, and that we would not and could not be satisfied and supremely happy without it. Upon the crucifixion and the resurrection of Jesus, one of the grandest principles of the Gospel depends. If children were taught this early in life, death would not have the horrifying influence that it does have over many childish minds." (*Juvenile Instructor, op. cit.*)

Perhaps this latter statement by President Smith is among the most intelligent statements that could be made to children about death.

After Mortality

Immortality
Hugh B. Brown

Recent poignant experiences have reminded some of us that a foundation stone of all religion is entwined with the thought of life beyond the grave, of the immortality of the soul, and of man's relationship to Deity. Sooner or later life's vicissitudes bring each of us to grips with this important subject, giving us cause to reevaluate our convictions, to reexamine our faith in this essentially spiritual aspect of our religion. Each of us, regardless of color, creed, or nationality, has a rendezvous with the experience that we call death.

The question of the immortality of the soul is the most persistent, the most universal inquiry of all time. It has in every age attracted the attention of the learned and the unlearned, the religious and irreligious, the rich and the poor. No other subject touches human welfare and human happiness so intimately.

The belief that the road of life merges into an endless freeway that leads to a more beautiful home and more fruitful life than any experience in mortality has been the inspiration of the great souls in all ages. This belief, older than the pyramids, antedating the first record of man's thoughts, has been firmly established in the minds and consciousness of the human race. There is a remarkable unanimity on this subject among the leaders throughout the ages, regardless of their adherence to other aspects of religion. This almost universal belief inspires hope, faith, and

Address delivered at the 137th Annual General Conference of the Church, April 1967. Published in *Improvement Era*, June 1967, pp. 26-28.

fortitude as we approach our turn to join that innumerable caravan and take our place in the sacred halls of death.

Revelation is unfolding truth whether in the test tube, the human mind, or message from the Creator. It is the infinite becoming known.

Death is not extinguishing the light, but is putting out the lamp, because the dawn has come. Night never has the last word. The dawn is irresistible. Both religion and science teach us that nothing is ever annihilated; forms change and patterns are altered. We do not even attempt to anticipate the details, but it is unreasonable to conclude that a law that operates everywhere else in life ceases to operate only in life's highest, noblest form—human personality. The human spirit shrinks from extinction. It refuses to believe that the departed have vanished like the flame of a burnt-out candle. There has never been an age in which the hope of life, immortal and eternal, has not flamed brightly.

In this world of indestructibility, each of us is a timeless, spaceless unit of energy. Is it not absurd to assume that the infinitesimal electron is of more import in the economy of the universe than the creative consciousness that is I?

If there are permanent values in the universe, it seems that human sympathy, love, mutual service among mankind, intellectuality, and spirituality—the highest and noblest qualities of which the human mind can conceive, qualities which have been produced at tremendous cost and sacrifice—must be permanent.

That the Savior conquered death, after having taken upon himself mortality, gives us the divine assurance that our spirits also transcend death and that our loved ones who have gone before still live. Our spirits are divine, for they are the offspring of Deity; therefore, our spirits cannot be touched by death. It was this transcendent thought that inspired the apostle Paul to say: "O death, where is thy sting? O grave, where is thy victory?" (1 Corinthians 15:55.)

Faintly we are beginning to discern the fact that the real world is the spiritual world, and that a spiritual civilization must spring from ruins of the old if man is to keep his place in the universe. Life is the absolute power that overrules all else. There can be no cessation. Man does not have the power to destroy life.

Our world is an interesting, beautiful, wonderful, increasingly intelligible place, and in many ways a delightful home, but the question will not be repressed: Does it have some significance beyond what is seen and temporal? Dare we think of a design connecting the antemortal, the mortal, and the postmortal?

The supreme appetite of man is for life—harmonious, eternal life. Nature provides for the complete fulfillment at some time or place of all of the appetites of man. The desire for immortality is the supreme, the eternal, the everlasting desire.

When I consult my own inner consciousness I find a deep-seated—in fact, an instinctive—feeling of immeasurable oldness, an echo of time immemorial, as well as a feeling of necessary endlessness. No logical reasoning can dispel these feelings. I did not put these feelings in my inner self; I found them there when I grew old enough to introspect my mind. In spite of recurring doubts and criticisms, there they have remained. If we believe in man's divine origin, we must conclude that mankind has a mission that cannot be encompassed in mortality; that power has a divine purpose that cannot be fully employed or utilized during earth life; that every faculty has a function, even though some are not in evidence in our earthly environment.

Each of us must someday face the question propounded by Job: "If a man die, shall he live again?" In other words, is the death of the body the finality of human existence? What becomes of the soul, the self—that intangible but very real essence we call personality? Does it vanish into nothingness?

The heart-hunger of mankind after immortality is instinctive within him, and like all other normal instincts is grounded in the structure of his being. The human spirit, by its very nature, has a passion for life—continuous life. It has eternity stamped upon its inner constitution, and it reflects in its hopes and dreams that which eternally is.

With the tremendous strides that science is making in

our day, there is dawning upon this age what might be termed a scientific spirituality—a new type of mind that studies the truths of faith with the care and caution and candor of science, yet keeping the warmth and glow and power of faith.

Spiritual insight is as real as scientific insight. Indeed, it is but a higher manifestation of the same thing. The saint as well as the scientist has witnessed the truth of reality. One may deem his knowledge revelation, and the other, intellectual conclusion, but in both cases it is insight—the conviction of reality.

That which impresses one most strongly in the teachings of Jesus is the fact that he did not argue. He stated the sublime truth of immortality of man as though it were an elementary fact that needed no argument to justify its acceptance.

Man, in his mortal state, is not a being completed and perfect. Rather, mortal life is a prenatal state, awaiting birth. As Franklin so truly said, "Life is rather a state of embryo, a preparation for life. A man is not completely born until he has passed through death."

Even the best of men, when they come to the end of their days, feel a keen sense of incompleteness. They have been unable to do what they dreamed and resolved they would do. May this not be a confirmatory suggestion that there is a design still to be carried out?

The mind of man is never satisfied with its accomplishments; it seems to be built upon a scale that only life eternal can satisfy. Perhaps this is what Browning meant when he said: ". . . a man's reach should exceed his grasp, or what's a heaven for?" (Robert Browning, "Andrea del Sarto.")

There may be and doubtless will be new conditions, new laws, new methods; but the essential soul will still have its faculties unimpaired—in fact, heightened and clarified—to pursue its quest for truth.

No bodily change, no earthly vicissitude affects the integrity and the permanence of the self. The spirit does not age with the body nor does it perish with the body. It is a divine effluence of reality, and as such must always persist.

The self, by its very nature, transcends mortality.

Victor Hugo left us a challenging reflection not long before he died. He said, "The nearer I approach the end the plainer I hear around me the immortal symphonies of the world which invites me. It is marvelous yet simple. For half a century I have been writing my thoughts in prose and in verse; history, philosophy, drama, romance, tradition, satire, ode and song; I have tried all. But I feel I have not said the thousandth part of what is in me. When I go down to the grave I can say like many others,—'I have finished my day's work.' But I cannot say, 'I have finished my life's work.' My day's work will begin again the next morning. The tomb is not a blind alley; it is an open thoroughfare. It closes on the twilight, it opens on the dawn. My work is only beginning; my work is hardly above the foundation. I could gladly see it mounting forever. The thirst for the infinite proves infinity."

When those eleven downhearted men suddenly became aware that Jesus was in their midst—the Jesus who only hours before had been scourged and stabbed on the hill—they, as Luke said, "believed not for joy." (See Luke 24:41.) It was too good to be true, and then came his marvelous challenge and demonstration as he said: ". . . handle me, and see; for a spirit hath not flesh and bones, as ye see me have.

"And when he had thus spoken, he showed them his hands and his feet." (Luke 24:39-40.) They saw; they touched, and were touched by his glorious resurrected body. That was the great revelation—Christ was real and touchable.

What I say here now reflects not only Bible study and prayerful meditation, but also actual experience that defies a thousand and one traditions and assumptions. I would not be standing here if it had not come to life within me when I was on the edge of my own abyss.

The hands, feet, and side of Christ had bled in the awful turning of his solitary winepress before they were pierced at Golgotha. His whole body bled in the midst of his vicarious pain. This was an actual experience; it was not a myth.

When the eleven apostles were celebrating an extended Easter at Jerusalem, they were overwhelmed by the implications of his final instructions and seemed moved by an endowment of the Spirit, for they witnessed not only his own unforeseen immortality but also their own immortality. It was the reality of reunion of their lives with his life; it was knowing him again, in their midst, being with them. It was his ministering, dining, sharing with them. It was being close—closer than ever before. They became aware of his great power—indeed, all power both in heaven and in earth had been given unto him.

We bear witness to these New Testament insights, the newest of which is his present touch. To be in touch with Christ means today what it meant to John and Peter and Paul: to see, to receive, and to prize the actual ministrations.

We witness that his voice, his person, has been manifested today in our time and culture. And more: that he will now, as then, manifest himself to those who will come as John came, not counting the cost. He can be and is touched by the power of his divine Sonship.

We bear witness that Christ was the revelation of God, the Father, and I dare proclaim what some creeds have forbidden us to say: that when the disciples knelt at Jesus' feet, embraced his knees, looked into his face, they were beholding and touching a personality who had become absolutely like the Eternal Father.

We bear witness that the touch of Christ, as he is presently glorified, is the touch of the highest nature of God. When he entered the presence of God, the Father, he was transformed into the express image of his person. He became not only the revelation of the Father but also the revelation of redeemed man.

Behold the vibrant Christ who manifests a love that does not flourish on distance, on utter unlikeness, on the removal of similitude! Union and communion—real kinship—are the sharing of all levels of experience.

Behold the Christ who knew all human sickness, that he might have compassion; who was healed and lifted up, that he might have healing and lifting power; who was glorified in the presence of the Father, that he might glorify the Father by glorifying us!

For this cause came he into the world; for this cause he voluntarily offered his life, broke the bands of death, was resurrected from the dead, vouchsafed to all men the blessings of the resurrection, and was glorified by the Father.

One of the best-attested facts in history is the fact of the resurrection of Jesus Christ. He said, ". . . I go [to] prepare a place for you, . . . that where I am, there you may be also." (John 14:3.) Paul tells us that "as in Adam all die, even so in Christ shall all be made alive." (1 Corinthians 15:22.) Hear Christ's inspiring message to Martha and to all the world: ". . . I am the resurrection, and the life: he that believeth in me, though he were dead, yet shall he live: And whosoever liveth and believeth in me shall never die." (John 11:25-26.)

With Job of old and with the apostles I humbly bear witness that I know that my Redeemer lives, and that he shall stand at the last day upon the earth. I bear this testimony humbly and faithfully, in the name of Jesus Christ. Amen.

A Future
Where Loved Ones Wait
Richard L. Evans

There were scenes of light and triumph, overcoming scenes of darkness, death, and despair. We often see people bereaved and wonder how they face the irrevocable fact. But they face it because life goes on, and because the fact is there to face. They face it with an awareness that all of us shall face this ultimate eventuality. We all one day leave life and loved ones, or our loved ones leave us, and we go on, calmly as we can, as we must, because we must. "In every . . . age the thoughts of men have traveled . . . beyond the narrow bounds of mortal life," wrote a distinguished writer, "and, while the mystery of death has been deeply and often tragically felt, it has never been accepted as a finality in human experience. . . . The tide of vitality in the heart and soul of man . . . sweeps past the mystery of death . . . into the undiscovered world beyond." (Editorial, *The Outlook,* March 29, 1902.) "How [then] shall we think of the dead? . . . I can tell you how I think of . . . [them]. I think that there are no dead; I think that there is no death; . . . that life goes on unbroken by what we call death. . . . I think of death as a glad awakening from this . . . life; . . . as a graduation from this primary department into some higher rank . . . of learning. I think of the dead as possessing a more splendid equipment for a larger life . . . than was possible to them on earth—a life in which I shall in due time join them if I am counted worthy of their fellowship in

"The Spoken Word" from Temple Square, presented over KSL and the Columbia Broadcasting System April 7, 1968. Copyright 1968. Reprinted in *Improvement Era,* June 1968, p. 109.

the life eternal." (Dr. Lyman Abbott.) It is this that sustains us as our loved ones leave—not the immortality of memory only, but the immortality of a literal personal continuance. And so we come again to a reaffirmation of faith—faith in the eternal continuance of truth, of intelligence, of personality, of progress—faith in the eternal plan and purpose of our Father, who made us in his own image, and whose intent it is that we should have everlasting life with our loved ones, with family and friends. As Henry de Lafayette Webster said, "There is a future, O thank God!"—a future where our loved ones wait.

J Day

Sterling W. Sill

Someone has said that the most important event in life is death. Death is the gateway to immortality. We live to die, and then we die to live. Ordinarily we don't like to think about death because it is associated with unpleasantness.

But death does not cease to exist merely because it is ignored. The ancient Egyptians had a much more logical procedure for handling this situation. On their important festive occasions they kept constantly on display before the revelers a great image of death. They wanted to remind themselves that someday they would die. Now I don't want to frighten anyone unduly here today, but I would just like to point out in passing that someday each one of us is going to die, and certainly one of the wisest ways to spend life is in an effective preparation for death.

Branch Rickey, the famous baseball manager, was once asked to name his greatest day in baseball. He replied, "I haven't had it yet." And I would like to invite you to consider this important question. How could you employ your life more constructively than in getting ready for those exciting experiences that you haven't yet had?

H. G. Wells gave us some stimulating self-improvement help, when many years ago he wrote an interesting fantasy entitled *The Time Machine.* Out of his imagination he invented a machine that could carry people through time much as an airplane carries us through space. In his time

Address delivered at the 134th Annual General Conference of the Church, April 1964. Published in *Improvement Era*, June 1964, pp. 465-67.

machine Mr. Wells could go thousands of years back into the past in just a few minutes. Being a historian he took great delight in witnessing the important events of history while they were actually taking place.

He made a trip back to the year 1066 to verify personally some of the details of the Battle of Hastings. Then he went still farther back for a visit in the Golden Age of Greece, and he personally discussed philosophy with Socrates 400 years B.C. With his mission completed, his time machine would bring him back into the present. Then by pushing the lever in the other direction, this time scientist could with equal speed go up into the future to study civilizations and institutions as they would someday actually be. And his speedometer always indicated which year of time he was in.

While this story is only a fantasy, it contains the germ of a great possibility. Actually our minds have been equipped with some significant time-traveling abilities. In thought, we can go backward or forward across time faster than any missile can travel through space. In President McKay's great book *Gospel Ideals,* he has one paragraph in which he says, "Last night I dreamed about my mother." And then he said, "I would like to dream about my mother more often." In his dream he went back into his own past and relived those important days at his mother's knee, when he learned the lessons of life that brought him to the presidency of the Church. Upon awaking he found that his ideals had been renewed and his ambitions greatly strengthened. He had revitalized his life by reabsorbing the original good from the greatest experiences of his own past.

Whether we refer to this process as reflection, meditation, or assimilation, a great source of strength may be had from reliving the past. An even greater source of strength can come from preliving the important events of our own futures. This ability to look ahead might be called vision or foresight or the utilization of that wonderful power of imagination, which is like a giant radar beam searching the skies of future years. Someone has said that one of the greatest gifts that God has ever given to man is an imagination.

When in our minds we pre-live our marriage, we help to determine the kind of person that we would like to be when that event arrives. As we pre-live our success, we develop the abilities necessary to bring it about. And with the information and direction given us in the Holy Scriptures we can even pre-live that important period that lies beyond the boundaries of this life.

In a very literal way, God has given important time-traveling abilities to the prophets; for example, Abraham was permitted to go back thousands of years into the past to review his own premortal existence and learn something about the purposes of God, even before this earth had been created. In telling of this experience Abraham said, "Now the Lord had shown unto me, Abraham, the intelligences that were organized before the world was; and among all these there were many of the noble and great ones;

"And God saw these souls that they were good, and he stood in the midst of them, and he said: These I will make my rulers; for he stood among those that were spirits, and he . . . said unto me: Abraham, thou art one of them; thou wast chosen before thou wast born.

"And there stood one among them that was like unto God, and he said unto those who were with him: We will go down, for there is space there, and we will take of these materials, and we will make an earth whereon these may dwell;

"And we will prove them herewith, to see if they will do all things whatsoever the Lord their God shall command them;

"And they who keep their first estate shall be added upon; and they who keep not their first estate shall not have glory in the same kingdom with those who keep their first estate; and they who keep their second estate shall have glory added upon their heads for ever and ever." (Abraham 3:22-26.)

Then when Abraham came back into his own present, he was more thoroughly fortified for his future adventure in life. On the other hand, Moses was permitted to preview the entire history of the earth from the beginning to the end thereof. On that memorable occasion when Moses met God face to face on the mount, he was given a great vision, in which he beheld all of the earth. The record says there was not a particle of it which he did not behold, discerning it by the Spirit of God: "And he beheld also the inhabitants thereof, and there was not a soul which he beheld not. . . ." (Moses 1:28.)

In large part the Holy Scriptures are made up of great revelations which God has caused to be written down for our use in preparation for those great days which we haven't yet had. For what advantage it may give us, just suppose that we practise pre-living our own resurrection. A recent newspaper article told of some Russian prisoners of war returning to their families after a twenty-year absence. We can imagine the pleasure of being reunited with loved ones after a long separation, but what a thrilling experience it will be to be reunited with ourselves.

We do not like to think about our spirits and bodies being even temporarily separated at death. But in the resurrection what will be the joy of the faithful when the spirit and the body will be inseparably joined together in celestial glory. Next to the human spirit, the human body is the greatest of all God's creations, without which we could never have a fulness of joy. Our spirits were begotten of God in heaven, and one of the most important purposes of our mortal lives is to be "added upon" with a body of flesh and bones.

This was also one of the important purposes of the earth life of Jesus. It has always been something of a mystery to me why some people are so insistent in depriving God, the greatest of all, of his body. This is especially hard to understand when we know that it was a part of the punishment for Lucifer's sin that he could never progress beyond the status of a spirit. If a body of flesh and bones were not necessary, it never would have been created in the first place. If it were not necessary for eternity, the resurrection never would have been instituted. If a body were not necessary for God the Father, then there would have been no point in God the Son being resurrected. Certainly a glorious resurrection day will be one of our most thrilling days.

One of the most important days of World War II was D

Day. D Day was a term used to indicate an unspecified day on which some crucial military operation was to take place. D Day in World War II was on June 6, 1944. That was the day on which the Allied Invasion Forces swarmed onto the beaches of Normandy to reestablish their foothold in western Europe. D Day was the beginning of the end of the World War II. August 15, 1945, was called "VJ Day" or Victory in Japan Day. But the day that will probably be the most exciting of all of our days will also be a "J Day" or Judgment Day.

This is a term frequently used in the scripture to indicate another unspecified day on which the most crucial operation of our existence will take place. This is the world's "settling-up day." It is the day when the books are going to be balanced. This is the day that the prophets have looked forward to and talked about since the world began. In the scripture this day has been called by various names including "The Day of Reckoning," "The Day of the Lord," "The Great and Terrible Day." For some it will be doomsday, but many scriptural passages mention this day as though it needed no qualifying phrase. They merely call it "The Great Day." It is very interesting that at any important race the spectators usually congregate at the finish line. And what could be more exciting than to be at the finish line in the race of life. This is another interesting reason why we should be ready for "J Day." In our own time the Lord has said, "Therefore . . . labor diligently . . . to bind up the law and seal up the testimony, and to prepare the saints for the hour of judgment which is to come." (D&C 88:84.)

We know quite a lot about "J Day," and apparently it is going to be quite a day. We know the purpose of Judgment Day. We know what action is contemplated. We know who will be in court. We know that God will be there. We know that all of us will be there. We know that all of the members of the Church will be there, and that all of the nonmembers of the Church will be there. Even Satan, and all of his angels will be there. The Prophet Jude said, "And the angels which kept not their first estate, but left their own habitation, he hath reserved in everlasting

chains under darkness unto the judgment of the great day."
(Jude 1:6.)

In an interesting "time-machine experience," John the
apostle was permitted actually to preview the judgment.
This revelation was of such great consequence that
thereafter he has been called John the Revelator. However,
this revelation was not given for John's benefit alone. The
Lord specifically instructed him to write down what he saw
so that we might see it also. John says that while he was in
the spirit on the Lord's day, he heard a voice behind him. It
was a great voice as of a trumpet "Saying, I am Alpha and
Omega, the first and the last: and, What thou seest, write in
a book, . . ." (Revelation 1:11.)

John says that he turned to see who spoke to him and he
saw ". . . one like unto the Son of man, clothed with a gar-
ment down to the foot, and girt about . . . with a golden
girdle.

"His head and his hairs were white like wool, as white
as snow; and his eyes were as a flame of fire;

"And his feet like unto fine brass, as if they burned in a
furnace; and his voice as the sounds of many waters."
(Revelation 1:13-15.)

This was such a glorious personage that John said, "And
when I saw him, I fell at his feet as dead. And he laid his
right hand upon me, saying unto me, Fear not; I am the first
and the last:

"I am he that liveth, and was dead; and behold, I am
alive forevermore . . . and have the keys of hell and of
death." (Revelation 1:17-18.)

What a tremendous point to have clearly in mind, that
the Redeemer is alive. And that he is alive forevermore.
During the last few hundred years, the world has been
flooded with the crucifix. It pictures a dead Christ upon a
cross of pain. But Christ did not remain upon the cross.
Neither is the tomb his dwelling place. He is alive, and he
has the keys of death and hell. He also has the keys of
eternal life and celestial glory. To make sure that we should
understand, this glorious being said to John, "Write the
things which thou hast seen, and the things which are, and
the things which shall be hereafter." (Revelation 1:19.)

Anciently men communicated with each other by means of pictures. Now we usually use words to express thought, but we still think in pictures. If someone tells us his experience, we can understand it best when in our mind's eye we can actually see him doing it. The movies and television have become popular because pictures are one of the best ways to get ideas into our minds. John didn't just get the facts about the judgment, he actually saw it as it will someday take place. Then he transmitted these ideas to us in words, so that we could reconstruct the picture in our own minds. How well we develop this mental picturing power will largely determine our future.

Former Prime Minister Disraeli once said, "Genius is the power to visualize the objective." This is especially true of eternal objectives. If we lack this ability, we will certainly have trouble. Recently a friend said to me, "I just can't see myself being active in the Church." Neither can he see himself getting down on his knees before God. There are some people who can't see the advantages of honesty or morality or complying with the other commandments of God. This is not because they lack eyes. What they lack is the picturing power of a great faith. It will help us to live more effectively if we project John's words upon the screen of our minds so that we will be able to see the picture of our greatest day as we will someday actually experience it.

John said, "And I saw the dead, small and great, stand before God; and the books were opened: and another book was opened, which is the book of life: and the dead were judged out of those things which were written in the books, according to their works.

"And the sea gave up the dead which were in it; and death and hell delivered up the dead which were in them: and they were judged every man according to their works." (Revelation 20:12-13.)

Even hell will be emptied for judgment day. The problem that troubles our civil courts is that those involved cannot frequently agree as to the facts. But probably no one will be disposed to argue on "J Day." If God could show Abraham a rerun of his experience before the earth was created and if he could show Moses the entire history of the world before it happened, we can be sure that he can show us every detail of our lives exactly as they took place, with nothing left out.

An ancient American prophet asks this important question. He said, ". . . can ye imagine yourselves brought before the tribunal of God with your souls filled with guilt and remorse, having a remembrance of all of your wickedness, yea, a perfect remembrance of all your wickedness, yea, a remembrance that ye have set at defiance the commandments of God?" (Alma 5:18.)

That calls for an important ability, and the best way to avoid possible tragedy is to focus our imagination upon "J Day" before we actually get there. We can be absolutely certain that we will all want to be a faithful, devoted, hardworking, enthusiastic, full tithepaying member of God's kingdom when we stand before the judgment bar. But we must get the impulse to faithfulness ahead of time; as someone has said that hell is "truth seen too late."

Concerning those who fail to pass the final test on "J Day," John says, "And whosoever was not found written in the book of life was cast into the lake of fire." (Revelation 20:15.) What an experience that is going to be!

Then for the benefit of the faithful, John says, "And I saw a new heaven and a new earth: for the first heaven and the first earth were passed away; and there was no more sea.

"And I John saw the holy city, [the] new Jerusalem coming down from God out of heaven, prepared as a bride adorned for her husband.

"And I heard a great voice out of heaven saying, Behold, the tabernacle of God is with men, and he will dwell with them and they shall be his people, and God himself shall be with them, and be their God.

"And God shall wipe away all tears from their eyes; and there shall be no more death, neither sorrow, nor crying, neither shall there be any more pain: for the former things are passed away.

"And he that sat upon the throne said, Behold, I make all things new. And he said unto me, Write: for these words are true and faithful.

"He that overcometh shall inherit all things; and I will be his God, and he shall be my son." (Revelation 21:1-7.)

My brothers and sisters, what a lot of thrilling experiences we haven't yet had! May God help us to be prepared for them when they arrive, I pray in the name of Jesus Christ. Amen.

After Death, What?

W. Cleon Skousen

Fifteen thousand more days to live!

This is the prospect—or remaining life span—for the average young adult today. It simply means that in 15,000 days will come a transitional experience called death, which sweeps each of us into a whole new dimension of cosmic reality. For countless years people have asked just what happens at death.

Now that the gospel has been restored, we have received a tremendous vista of knowledge concerning life after death. We know that the separation of the spirit from the body is a very necessary part of God's plan and not a major tragedy, as many had supposed. What we call death is simply the temporary separation of the spirit from the body so that the spirit can be prepared for the resurrection. We are told that this is done in a place just outside our own dimension of reality, a place called the spirit world.

Preparation for the resurrection involves discipline, evaluation, reform, and hard work. For a certain few the transition from mortality to the resurrection can be accomplished in the "twinkling of an eye" (see D&C 63:51 and 101:31), but for all the rest extensive preparation is required.

God's justice requires that all be given an opportunity to hear and embrace the gospel plan for happy living. Since many persons never received that opportunity here on earth, they will have such an opportunity in the spirit

From *Improvement Era*, July 1969, pp. 72-75.

world. Even those who did hear the gospel here on earth
will apparently find many things to be done in the spirit
world before they are ready for the resurrection. The spirit
world, therefore, is an essential and busy interval in our
preparation for the future eternities.

It is also in the spirit world that each personality is
eventually judged and a determination made concerning
the degree of eternal glory to which that individual is
entitled. A modern revelation indicates that at the time of
its resurrection, each spirit is elevated to whatever degree
of glory it has earned. For example, speaking of those who
are celestial spirits, the Lord says, ". . . and *your* glory shall
be that glory by which your bodies are quickened." (D&C
88:28. Italics added.)

Thus, those who can be elevated to a celestial glory will
receive celestial bodies; those who cannot abide such a
glory will be given either terrestrial or telestial bodies, depending upon the level of glory their spirits are worthy to
receive.

It was Jesus who said, "In my Father's house are many
mansions" (John 14:2), but only in the writings of the
apostle Paul and in modern scripture do we have direct
reference to the fact that mankind will be resurrected to a
variety of glories, depending upon their worthiness. This
means that there must be different kingdoms designed to
accommodate people of different glories. In other words,
our human family will not all be together in the eternities.
Here is the way Paul describes it:

"There are also celestial bodies, and bodies terrestrial:
but the glory of the celestial is one, and the glory of the terrestrial is another, and the telestial is another. [This last
phrase appears only in the Joseph Smith Translation.]

"There is one glory of the sun, and another glory of the
moon, and another glory of the stars: for one star differeth
from another in glory.

"So also is the resurrection of the dead. . . ." (1 Corinthians 15:40-42.)

Paul was very obscure in discussing the origin of this
knowledge, because when it was revealed to him it included many things that he said were "not lawful for a man

to utter." (2 Corinthians 12:4.) In fact, the vision in which Paul received this information is treated so modestly in his writings that one has to analyze them very carefully to realize he is talking about himself. He said:

"I knew a man in Christ above fourteen years ago . . . such an one caught up to the third heaven. And I knew such a man . . . how that he was caught up into paradise, and heard unspeakable words, which it is not lawful for a man to utter. Of such an one will I glory: yet of myself I will not glory. . . ." (2 Corinthians 12:2-5.)

As a result of this magnificent revelation, Paul gave us his famous teachings on the resurrection and made specific reference to the different glories we will inherit according to our worthiness. Nevertheless, the details were left obscure, and it was not until modern times that we gained a thrilling and comprehensive understanding of the things Paul had seen.

It was on February 16, 1832, while Joseph Smith was residing at the Johnson home in Hiram, Ohio, that he and Sidney Rigdon unexpectedly received a vision of the glories similar to the one received by Paul. [This vision is recorded as section 76 in the Doctrine and Covenants.] As far as we know, Paul never recorded the details of that which he was shown, but Joseph Smith states that the modern vision had barely begun when "the Lord commanded us that we should write the vision." (D&C 76:28.)

Once this definitive revelation had been given concerning the resurrection, many other revelations (both ancient and modern) began to take on a whole new dimension of highly significant meaning. It not only demonstrated the literal reality of the "many mansions" referred to by the Savior, but it also revealed extremely important information concerning the kind of people who will go to each of these various glories or kingdoms.

We are told first of all that the celestial kingdom belongs to all those who accept the gospel of Jesus Christ without undue procrastination. (See D&C 76:51-53.)

Verses 71 to 79 [of section 76] state that if a person has an opportunity to embrace the fullness of the gospel during earth life but postpones accepting it until he reaches the spirit world, then he cannot be an heir to the celestial kingdom. He drops down to the next level, the terrestrial. Of course, if a person never even hears the gospel until he reaches the spirit world (and that has been the case with the majority of mankind), then he can accept it in the spirit world without any penalty, provided he would have accepted it in the flesh. In due time the ordinance work will be done for him vicariously (such as baptism for the dead referred to by Paul in 1 Corinthians 15:29), and then that person will be resurrected to the celestial glory just as though he had accepted the gospel while in earth life.

Modern revelation has further disclosed that the celestial kingdom is divided into three heavens or degrees. (D&C 131:1.) To attain the highest degree, one must be married for time and eternity by the power of God's holy priesthood. (D&C 131:2-3.) Only those who qualify for this highest discipline enjoy a continuing family relationship in the eternal worlds. (D&C 132:19.) And only those who qualify for this level will have the privilege of being tutored to follow in the footsteps of the Father and share in his infinite power. (D&C 132:20.) To these the Father says he will give "all things." Then the scripture adds, "They are they who are priests and kings, who have received of his fulness, and of his glory. . . . Wherefore, as it is written, they are gods, even the sons of God." (D&C 76:55-56, 58.)

Much of this, of course, is presently beyond rational comprehension. Paul warned us after receiving his great revelation that "eye hath not seen, nor ear heard, neither hath entered into the heart of man, the things which God hath prepared for them that love him." (1 Corinthians 2:9. See also Isaiah 64:4.)

But what about those who do not reach the celestial kingdom?

Paul pointed out that the terrestrial glory is of a different order and definitely inferior to that of the celestial kingdom, even as the moon is far less glorious than the brilliant illumination of the sun. (1 Corinthians 15:41-42.) Modern revelation has verified the accuracy of Paul's statement. (See D&C 76:70-71.)

As we have already mentioned, this is the kingdom

where the Father's children go who have had a chance to embrace the gospel and help establish the kingdom of God on earth, but who have passed by the opportunity and have not come forward to receive the plan of salvation until they reached the spirit world. (D&C 76:74.) They will enjoy a great glory, but it is far less than what they might have had.

These include that class of persons who are basically honorable men and women, but who have passed by the gospel of Jesus Christ by allowing themselves to be deceived by the craftiness of the philosophies of men. (D&C 76:75.) They were too sophisticated for anything so humble and simple as the gospel plan. In the spirit world they recognize their mistake, and, as the scales of their blindness, pride, and man-made illusions crumble away, they come forth at last to drink at the one glorious fountain whose living waters are such that the recipient need never thirst again. These have come lately, but at least they have come. Theirs is the glory of the moon.

In the parable of the ten virgins, the Lord suggests that in the terrestrial kingdom will be found some of those who have professed to be his followers. What has happened to them?

It seems they were not valiant. They did not keep their lamps lighted. They are likened unto five foolish virgins. When the Father needed them to help save more of their brothers and sisters, they did not come. They were slothful, waiting to be commanded in all things. They did not openly fight against the Church; they just let others do all the work, go on all the missions, serve in all the jobs of teachers and officers in the kingdom, pay all the tithes, take care of all the poor, administer to all the sick, visit all the orphans and widows and those in prison. In the heat of God's great battle against his apostate son Lucifer, they let others carry the burden of the fight. They stood back when they should have stood up—for freedom, for righteousness, for truth.

These are they of whom Christ will say at his coming, "Verily I say unto you, I know you not." (See Matthew 25:8-12.)

Last of all come those who go to the lowest of all of God's kingdoms. This is the glory telestial.

One unusual thing about this kingdom is the fact that all of the people assigned to this dimension are not of the same glory. Collectively, they are similar, even as the stars in the firmament are similar when compared with the luster of the moon or the magnificent glory of the sun. Nevertheless, individually they differ in glory as "one star differs from another." (D&C 76:98.)

These are they who did not embrace the fullness of the gospel of Jesus Christ when it came to them. (See D&C 76:101.) They gloried in the infatuating doctrines concocted by the imagination of men and "received not the gospel, neither the testimony of Jesus, neither the prophets, neither the everlasting covenant." (D&C 76:99-101.)

When the glory of the Savior is manifest, these will bow the knee and confess that he is the Christ. (See D&C 76:110.)

The telestial kingdom will include all those who have spent their lives in profligate living without the slightest virtue of repentance in this life. The Lord says these are they who are liars, sorcerers, adulterers, whoremongers, and whosoever loves and makes a lie. (See D&C 76:103.)

These are they who will not be gathered with the Saints nor caught up in the cloud to meet the Lord when he comes. (D&C 76:102.) These are they who suffer the wrath of God on earth. (D&C 76:104.) These are they who suffer the vengeance of eternal fire while they are waiting in the spirit world. (D&C 76:105.) Unfortunately, these are as innumerable as the stars in the firmament of heaven or as the sand upon the seashore. (D&C 76:109.)

The most that any of these can expect in the vast reaches of eternity will be their role as "servants of the Most High." This means they can never achieve godhood. (D&C 76:112.) Where Christ and the Father dwell they cannot go, "worlds without end." (D&C 76:112.)

These are they who, when they die, must remain with Lucifer and his angels until the end of the millennium, when they are resurrected as third-class citizens in the eternities of God's great cosmos. (D&C 76:84-85.)

One of the most astonishing passages in modern revelation on the resurrection informs us that the very least of

God's kingdoms—the telestial glory—is so magnificent that it *"surpasses all understanding."* (D&C 76:89. Italics added.)

This means that God, in his mercy and anxiety for our welfare, has prepared a series of glorious kingdoms, the *least* of which is too marvelous for us to imagine.

And if such superlatives apply to the minimal glory of the kingdom like unto the stars, what of the kingdom of glory like unto the moon? And, even more importantly, what can be said of the supreme exaltation of them all, the glory like unto the sun?

It is this highest degree of the highest glory for which the restored gospel of Jesus Christ is specifically designed to prepare us. Among all of God's endowments, this is the most glorious. At this stage of our development, none of us could be given more. And knowing as much as we do of the coming resurrection, who would dare aspire to anything less?

Each day we make decisions that help determine our place in the eternities. Our task is to live the kind of lives that will make it possible for us to win the supreme prize— the fullness of the glory of the sun—the highest degree of the celestial kingdom.

The Final Awakening

Richard L. Evans

Recently we recalled a scene from *The Blue Bird* by Maurice Maeterlinck as the children leave their home in heaven to be born on earth, with anxiety and anticipation, some not wanting to leave their friends, some fearing to come to earth. Then there was the sound of gladness, the song of mothers coming out to meet the children sent from their heavenly home. Suppose now we follow through a further sequence suggested by this scene—through the living and learning of life, with its problems and opportunities, its choosing and growing, its doing and enduring and understanding—and then after all the experiences of earth there comes a return to the heavenly home—again with anxiety and anticipation and with reluctance to leave friends and family. Leaving where we lived before and coming here we call birth. Leaving here and going on to the other opportunities we call death, one being as natural and essential as the other. And how blessed it is to have the sense of assurance that reunion with friends and family is a part of our Father's plan and purpose, as we leave this life with an everlasting future before us. And there the knowledge of our premortal past and of life's ever-continuing purpose will give us the answers we so much seek, with full meaning to our memories. Scripture gives us this assurance. Our own conviction within our souls gives us this assurance. God our Father has not planned for us to

"The Spoken Word" from Temple Square, presented over KSL and the Columbia Broadcasting System, May 31, 1964. Copyright 1964. Reprinted in *Improvement Era*, August 1964, p. 684.

pass fleetingly into a nothingness, through the swift little-
ness of mortal life, but has given us truth and intelligence
and the awareness of ourselves and the love of loved ones
and life as an everlasting literal reality. "Is death the last
sleep?" asked Sir Walter Scott. And then he answered his
own question: "No, it is the last and final awakening." And
to those who have lost those they love: May the acuteness
of sorrow be softened by the assurance that these things are
so, and that life is worth all the doing and enduring, and
that beyond time there is eternity with continued consciousness and purpose and a literal reality of resurrection—with a continuing personal awareness as real as we
have here. You who mourn and you who remember, take
comfort to your hearts this day—and always with the
assurance that these things are so.

Section 6

Remembering
Our
Dead

An Incident of Everyday Life

Edward H. Anderson

Another death at the hospital! The nurse said it was James L. Peck. He came from somewhere out near Mill Creek, but no one seemed to know much about him. He was not old, and though he had been sick for months, and in the hospital for some weeks, he was one of the patients that did not himself expect to pass away.

For want of better connections, an undertaker was phoned for, and, with an eye to business, he communicated with the United States Surveyor General, in whose service, it was learned, Peck had been engaged for over nine years, until he was taken so sick, in October 1904, that he had been compelled to ask for a leave of absence. This was granted, without pay, and extended, two or three times, by the Commissioner of the General land office. The last extension was to expire July 31, 1905.

"No; The government does not provide for the burial of its employees, in case of death," said the officer to the undertaker. "We have helped individually in some cases, but it will not be necessary in this case, for he had property enough for that."

On several occasions, when friends from the office had visited him, Peck had expressed the hope that on the expiration of his leave he would be back at his desk again. He was an engineer of splendid ability. Until his sickness began to wear on him, none were brighter. When the plats bore his initials, there was no need for the chief to worry

From *Improvement Era*, May 1905, pp. 823-26.

further about the calculations—the areas were perfect, if
J.L.P. was marked thereon.

"Peck is dead." "Peck is dead," flew from phone to
phone, on the night of July 19, 1905. First to the chief clerk,
then to all the clerks who could be reached. "He died at the
hospital, this afternoon, and will be buried tomorrow
afternoon at 2 o'clock. Poor Peck, he is better off!"

Promptly at two, at the funeral chapel, a little company had gathered to pay their last respects. Ten of the
nineteen present were from the office. The wife and three
children were present. The bishop had been asked to
conduct the service, but there were no singers, and in
fifteen minutes it was all over; for little was known of him
who lay dead, and there was not much to say. His work, his
toil, his devotion to duty, were mostly hidden in the government township plats.

Six of his fellow clerks carried the casket to the hearse.
Several little hand bouquets of flowers, and a wreath of
white carnations, inscribed "From friends in the office," lay
upon it; then the hearse and the family carriage set off to
the cemetery at a rapid gait. People looked up from the
busy street and said: "Somebody dead!" and passed on
about their tasks unmoved.

The cemetery lies upon the hillsides, northeast of the
city, overlooking the whole green valley. There are lovely
lawns and flowerbeds, at the entrance. There are green lots,
marble headstones, costly monuments, trees and foliage,
but this procession bore up, and up, until the scorched
mountain areas lay all about—still up the barren hills.
There are only single-grave lots here; long rows of wooden
headboards stretch up in tiers, separated only by narrow,
sunburned spaces where the June-grass lies scorched of the
sun, and the gray sage tells its tale of thirst.

At length, at the extreme end of one of these tiers, the
panting horses halt. The open grave is ready. The casket is
taken by four office friends from the hearse. The flowers are
laid aside, revealing the word "Father," in shining letters,
on the casket lid. Then the four friends let down the sealed
wooden box into parched mother earth, amid the children's
and the widow's sobs and tears.

A friend is asked to pray: "We dedicate, O God, this grave, as the resting place of our friend and fellow workman. May his body rest in peace; may this place be sacred to his name and memory; may he arise with the just on the resurrection day, in Jesus' name. Amen."

While the workmen, in seeming lack of both sentiment and feeling, shovel the earth into the open grave, I turn to read the names on the line of wooden headboards.

Here is one on whose spot of earth the flowers are scarcely faded, whose grave is trodden upon by the friends who show respect to his nearest neighbor. Whose name? Joseph H. Ward! editor, publisher, author, poet, only five days dead! And so he lies here!

Only Sunday last, and perhaps ten thousand children sang the words of his songs; and the organs of a hundred Sabbath Schools will peal forth, next Sunday, in memory of the pioneers, his "Utah, the Queen of the West." *And he lies here!*

So quickly are we ready to return? But before the door of the carriage closed, standing with these thoughts in my mind, I grasped a clear and full glimpse of the scene about me. The salt sea, shining in the hot sun of the west; the cool canyons of the Wasatch; the gray, barren, rough pinnacles of the majestic Cottonwoods; the Jordan, winding its sluggish way to the lake; the city, a thousand feet below, hidden in the shade of its ten thousand trees, with its people's pleasures, struggles, ambitions, and schemes! After all, what could be more appropriate and beautiful than a final heritage here, overlooking these scenes?

And here, and so, rest my friends, the engineer and the poet! As in life they modestly towered over many, so in death they sleep above us all. Strangers in life; in death, neighbors, their narrow homes side by side!

One of the clerks turned and said: "Of what use is effort and struggle for knowledge and ability, with such an end?"

And well may one ask: "Shall the house of talent, the temple of keen and educated intellect and great ability, so end, and rest unrecognized, neglected and forgotten?"

But it is only seeming neglect and forgetfulness. I have hope of everlasting life. The personal earth-struggle which ripens the soul with rich experience is recompense even for such an end: for grass, and trees, and lawns, and flowers, and costly monuments, and stately pomp, and weeping multitudes, in their turn, shall pass away; but the rich scholarship of the soul lives on with it forever.

The carriage rolled quickly down the slopes, and we were soon lost in the city's crowds, rush and routine.

Two Ways
to Remember the Dead

Hugh Nibley

On Memorial day we think of our dead and put flowers on their graves. Is there anything more we can do? Many like to think that the dead enjoy a kind of continued existence by living in our memories. That is a kindly sentiment but more depressing than exhilarating. It has the faint odor and faded colors of a Maeterlinck fantasy or a Russian novel (such as *Obmolov's Dream*), and it meets us often in the wistful and heartbreaking little epitaphs that have been found on the graves of pagan Greeks and Romans. To think constantly of the dead is morbid; to think of them occasionally is nice—but a poor sort of immortality. We have occasionally used the expression "earth-bound." Things of the spirit should not be earth-bound. What could be more depressing than the old-fashioned churchyard with its shadowy vaults; its seeping damp and odor of decay; its aged, mossy stones; its weeping willows and drooping plumes; in short, all those fixtures of the cult of the dead which seem like nothing so much as desperate devices to tie the dead to this world and keep them always within call.

This Gothic view of death, this obsession with the grisly remnants of the body, is not a healthy thing. The reaction from it in modern times has been a flight to another and equally unhealthy extreme, for the present age seems determined to leave death out of its calculations entirely, save for certain annoying details of a sanitary and legal nature. This has done much to make for shallowness and triviality

From *The World and the Prophets,* Deseret Book Co., 1954, pp. 149-56.

in modern life. We think and act as if death were not part of the program at all, or as if it were a frightful piece of bungling in the ordering of our lives, a terrible and senseless mistake. Death has disappeared from our serious thinking to meet us in every drugstore and bus station as the leitmotif of all our lighter reading. A strange and sordid business, this preoccupation with the sensational, the sordid, and the brutal aspects of death. The spectre which we drove out the back door has returned by the front.

How then should one think of the dead? It is one of the offices of true religion to teach us that. It was because philosophy could not answer the great questions of life, as we have seen, that such men as Clement and Justin and Tertullian turned from it to Christianity. Speculation and tradition, then as now, gave dignified but quite unsatisfactory answers, and the honest seeker saw clearly that if men were ever to learn anything certain about the great mysteries of the beyond, such information would have to come by revelation. That is true today as it was in ancient times. The comfort of philosophy, the quiet resignation and calm acquiescence with fate are well enough in themselves, but they are what in ancient times distinguished the pagan from the Christian, for the latter amazed the world by the robust and joyful assurance with which he viewed things of the other world. One of the most striking features of primitive Christianity was its constant and hardheaded insistence on the nearness and reality of the other side. A pagan critic of the early Christians remarked with wonder and annoyance that "they think nothing of present torments, but worry about what is to happen hereafter; and while they dread perishing *after* death, they don't fear dying here at all, so completely taken in are they by the false hope of living hereafter."[1] In *Androcles and the Lion,* George Bernard Shaw attempted to depict the odd and intriguing phenomenon of people who did not fear death; he saw that the contrast of this point of view with the normal one is so great as to create in itself hilarious situations; he saw that without any irreverence, there was something perfectly delightful in a religion which could view the life to come without any of the sombre Mumbo Jumbo of cult practices;

and he also realized that in the primitive Christian church he found a view of death that was unique in history and totally unlike that of the later Christian churches.

Now there is nothing unusual in a belief in an after life—as St. Augustine observed, it was a view quite commonly held by pagan philosophers. What set the early Christians apart was that they were not at all vague about the business. Just as for them the charismatic gifts—prophecy, tongues, healings, etc.—were real, literal, and concrete, so the life to come was not an abstraction or a rational necessity, but a thing to be experienced. As long as we find living prophets in the church, these things cannot be thought of as anything but real; they are all part of the same picture and have the same explanation—a living bond with the heavens, a continuous intercourse between this world and the other. And when the gift of prophecy departs, we witness at the same time the cessation of the other heavenly gifts, and with that the church changes its views of the other world, becoming perplexed and uncertain about things which it once knew so well.

A good deal has been written recently about the abrupt and surprising reorientation of the Christian church in the second century. At that time the attitude of the Christians to this world and the next suddenly and completely changed. So complete was this change of outlook and belief and so different was the resulting church from the apostolic one that the radical Dutch and German schools of church history were able to maintain that the primitive Christian church had never really existed, but was just an idealized reconstruction made in retrospect! One of the most instructive aspects of that change is the attitude of the church writers toward death. If we compare, say, Ignatius of Antioch with St. Basil on this subject, we find that the two men have absolutely nothing in common. Ignatius who lived in the first and early second centuries is straining every nerve to get to the other side. Any fame he might leave behind him as a saint or a martyr—any help he might give the church as its best-informed bishop—is no concern of his. As far as this world is concerned, he has lost all interest, every speck of it. Food and drink and the pleasure of

life have ceased to exist for him: "I no longer wish to live
after the manner of men," he writes to the Romans,
"believe me, I am sincere in this."[2] Though he is quite
aware that no man on earth could do the church as much
good as he by continuing to live, he is none the less resolved
not to linger here below for another moment if by any
means short of suicide he can leave it. For Ignatius, the
only reality is on the other side, and there is nothing
metaphysical or abstract about it.

But consider St. Basil, the great theologian of the fourth
century. Among his numerous surviving letters are a pair
written to console friends of his for the loss of a child.[3]
These consolations read exactly like those of the pagan
classical writers: The usual commonplaces about the inevitability of death and the shortness and misery of life do not
attempt to hide the conviction that death is after all the
supreme evil. But for a few scattered and conventional Biblical terms, the letters might have all been written by
Cicero, and some of them betray not the slightest trace of
any Christian influence. What had happened to the faith? I
grant you the *consolatio* was a well-established literary
genre in the schools, but Basil is writing to his dearest
Christian friends to give them what comfort he can as a
bishop—surely, if he had more to give them he would.
When the great Boethius in the sixth century was
condemned to die, it was not religion but Dame Philosophy
who brought him consolation in the death cell, and the famous essay she dictated on that melancholy occasion is not
to be distinguished from the writings of a typical heathen
philosopher in style, vocabulary, mood, or thought.
Eventually the Christians ended up fearing death more
anxiously than ever the pagans had. According to F. J. E.
Raby, by the end of the Middle Ages "it now became a
pious exercise to meditate on every ghastly detail which the
imagination could add to the picture of the Passion," the
individual identifying himself as much as possible with the
suffering.[4] "For the medieval Christian," writes Raby, "the
Day of Judgment was almost wholly a day of terror," and
"this same sense of terror is expressed in the . . . Mass for
the Dead. . . . The recurring refrain in this noble prose adds

to the sense of fear and apprehension."[5] This, Raby finds to be in complete contrast to "the joy and comfort of the early church."[6] And so we see, when revelation ceased, the Christians went back to thinking about death exactly as the pagans do. That is neither surprising nor reprehensible, but it does offer us a good test for a true and prophetic religion. For such a religion must surely be one in which the early rather than the later Christian view of death prevails, and such a view has always characterized the Latter-day Saints.

In the time that remains, I would like to point to one of the most wonderful and exciting aspects of the restored gospel, and that is the great work for the dead that is so peculiar to the Church of Jesus Christ. I do not specify "of Latter-day Saints," for this work was done by the primitive Christians as well. The knowledge of that all-important work was taken away at an early time, for after the third century the fathers of the church are much perplexed whenever it is mentioned though all admit that the earliest Christians actually did perform certain ordinances for the salvation of the dead. Furthermore, there is ample evidence that the Christians of apostolic times placed great emphasis on this work, for among the very early fragments of Christian literature that have been discovered in recent years, the subject is referred to as a very special knowledge imparted by the Lord to the Apostles in secret conferences after the resurrection.[7] This is not surprising, in view of the evidence of the Clementine homilies that the earliest Christians baptized in secret places,[8] and the constant charges of secrecy that were being brought against them—charges which they did not deny.

What was the nature of this work for the dead? The early Christians were convinced, as modern Christians are, that no man can get into heaven without baptism. Now most of those early Christians were converts to the church, and that meant that their parents in most cases and their grandparents in all cases had died without ever having heard of the baptism of salvation. Would these loved ones be forever damned? One of the first things Clement asks Peter upon being introduced to him, in the *Clementine Recognitions* is, "Shall those be wholly deprived of the kingdom of heaven who died before Christ's coming?" for he was thinking probably of his own forebears. Peter's answer is very significant: "You force me, Clement, to make public things that are not to be discussed. But I see no objection to telling you as much as we are allowed to. Christ, who always was from the beginning, has visited the righteous of every generation (albeit secretly), and especially those who have looked forward to his coming, to whom he often appeared. Still it was not yet time for the resurrection of bodies that perished then . . . but those who pleased him and did his will were translated to paradise, to be preserved there for the kingdom, while those who were not able to fulfil the complete law of justice, but had certain traces of carnal weakness in their nature, when their bodies died went in the spirit to be retained in good and happy places, that at the resurrection of the dead each might be empowered to receive an eternal heritage for the good he had done."[9] This much Peter is willing to tell, but he will not divulge to the new investigator just how those who have never heard the gospel in life are to be saved.

Whatever one may think of this very old fragment, it certainly shows that there were some early Christians who knew about salvation for the dead as a doctrine not taught to the general public. Both the theory and practice were remembered in the traditions of the church, where they provided no end of puzzlement and speculation to the commentators. Typical is St. Bruno at the end of the twelfth century who still recalls, with routine disapproval, of course, that certain of the early Christians in New Testament times "would baptize themselves in the place of a dead parent who had never heard the gospel, thereby securing the salvation of a father or a mother in the resurrection."[10] It might be argued that this work ceased in later times because after everybody had belonged to the church for generations there would be no unbaptized fathers and mothers. But one only need consider that in every age the church has been a missionary organization—a believing minority determined to carry forth the work of converting the heathen majority all of whose parents and grandparents are without baptism—to realize that work for the dead never should have ceased since it is necessary as long as outsiders continue to join the church. When a Germanic king was converted to Christianity, for example, he refused to accept baptism since that meant basely leaving his noble ancestors to suffer in hell while he enjoyed himself in heaven—that, in all conscience, he could not do.

From the earliest fragments, a good deal of the theory and practice of baptism for the dead in the apostolic church can be reconstructed. There were two main steps necessary to achieving salvation for the dead—the *kerygma* and baptism. The *kerygma* is the preaching of the word to those who are dead. It takes place, of course, in the other world, in a place where the dead are retained, a place designated with calculated vagueness—scrupulous avoidance of any attempt to designate a particular locale. What is made perfectly clear is that the dead who have not accepted the gospel on earth for any reason are detained in a place which is by no means disagreeable but is not heaven. To these, (the ancient saints taught), the Lord and, following his example, the Apostles and other holy men of old went down and preached the word.[11] No spirit was forced to accept the *kerygma* but such as did could leave their detention and advance in eternity just as soon as they had received the *seal*. The *seal* was what the early Christians called baptism in this connection. It was the seal of baptism that was put on the acceptance of the preaching on the other side. If it was accepted, the seal was effective, and what was sealed on earth was sealed in heaven. The seal was given by ministrants acting by proxy for the dead on this earth, for baptism could be given nowhere else, it was realized, and in no other way—"there is only one baptism," was the formula. In the *Pastor of Hermas* these earthly officiants are described as being the Apostles themselves, who while they were still alive baptized each other "for those who had fallen asleep before."[12]

Today, members of The Church of Jesus Christ of Latter-day Saints are everywhere engaged in the great work of searching out the records of their ancestors. Along with this the building and operation of our temples goes forward, for as in the ancient church, this work is not carried out in public. In these holy places the ordinances for the dead are performed by any worthy member of the Church who wishes to participate, from the age of eight years to extremely advanced ages when people are commonly thought to have passed their usefulness in most fields of work. Everything is done in a joyful and happy spirit. We love our kindred dead, and our own exaltation as well as theirs depends on the work we do for them. The New Revised Translation of the New Testament, recently greeted in many parts with considerable enthusiasm, gives an enlightening twist to the famous passage in 1 Corinthians 15:29 dealing with this work: "Else what shall they do which are baptized for the dead, if the dead rise not at all? why are they baptized for *their* dead?"

With the exception of the verse just cited, a few perplexed commentaries on it, and the unnoticed passage from the *Pastor of Hermas,* all our evidence for the practice of baptism for the dead in ancient times comes from fragments recently discovered. The possession of this strange and wonderful thing by the restored Church of Jesus Christ for over a hundred years would therefore seem to be an almost foolproof certificate of authenticity. The prophets of modern times remember the dead exactly as did those prophets of old, and in the growing evidence for the nature of that work among the first Christians, time has vindicated the modern prophets.

---

1. Minucius Felix, *Octavius,* c. viii.
2. Ignatius, *Letter to the Romans,* 2, 4, 7.
3. Basilius, *Epist. Class I,* 5, 6. (In *Patrologia Graec. XXXII,* 237-44.)
4. F. J. E. Raby, *Christian-Latin Poetry* (Oxford: Clarendon, 1927), pp. 420ff.
5. Ibid., pp. 445f.
6. Ibid., p. 444.
7. For a preliminary treatment of this subject, see Hugh Nibley, "Baptism for the Dead in Ancient Times," *Improvement Era,* 52 (1949): 24ff.
8. *Holilia Clementina* no. xiv, in *Patrologia Graec. II,* 345.
9. *Clementine Recognitions I,* 52 (*Patrologia Graec. I,* 1236).
10. St. Bruno, *Expos, in ep. I ad Cor xv 29* (*Patrologia Lat. CLIII,* 209); for the perplexities of the later fathers, see Nibley, *op. cit.,* 52 (1949): 91ff.
11. Nibley, *op cit.,* 52 (1949): 24ff.
12. *Hermae Pastor* III, Simil. IX, 16; cf. Nibley, *op. cit.,* 52 (1949): 90.

Answers
to
Gospel
Questions

Are the Dead Called Home?

Joseph Fielding Smith

QUESTION: *From time to time we hear speakers at funerals state that God had called the dead person home, which is the reason for that person's death. We are trying to harmonize the doctrine of free agency with this statement, but find difficulty in doing so. Is there any help you can give?*

ANSWER: One of the greatest blessings given to mankind is the gift of free agency. Without it there could be no salvation. It was Satan's plan to take away from the spirits assigned to come to this earth this great eternal blesssing. Under false pretenses he offered to save all the children of our Eternal Father, without any exception, on the terms that our Eternal Father would surrender his throne to him. Such a salvation would have required each individual to surrender his divine gift of freedom of thought and action, therefore it could be no salvation at all. With the divine privilege of accepting or rejecting the eternal plan which had been prepared, each soul is placed in the category of freedom of action and will. Hence each soul is subject to the rewards and punishment based on individual conduct.

One of the great commandments is as follows: "Honour thy father and thy mother: that thy days may be long upon the land which the Lord thy God giveth thee." (Exodus 20:12.)

Paul commenting on this said: "Children, obey your parents in the Lord: for this is right. Honour thy father and

From *Answers to Gospel Questions*, Deseret Book Co., 1960, 3:46-48.

mother; which is the first commandment with promise; That it may be well with thee, and thou mayest live long on the earth." (Ephesians 6:1-3.)

In giving counsel to the Corinthian Saints, who had been guilty of violating the sacred observance of the sacrament, Paul further said: "For he that eateth and drinketh unworthily, eateth and drinketh damnation to himself, not discerning the Lord's body. For this cause many are weak and sickly among you, and many sleep." (1 Corinthians 11:29-30.)

Evidently Paul meant that many had passed away because of their violation of this commandment. There can be little question raised contrary to the fact that men shorten their lives by violation of the commandments of the Lord. The use of narcotics, liquors, and other drugs and stimulants inevitably weakens and impairs the functions of the body, thus shortening the span of life.

Even good, faithful persons, who disregard the laws of health, may shorten the life span which otherwise could have been theirs. Moreover, we are all subject to the ravages of disease, disaster, accidents that could, and often do, shorten life.

Nearly every day we read of innocent persons dying in automobile accidents, by drowning in some stream or lake, or in some other danger, death has overtaken them, and it was no fault of their own. We are all subject to the various vicissitudes and conditions in life which confront us which could not be foreseen. It would be contrary to sound thinking to assume that the Lord has decreed that these individuals had been called home by such accidents or calamities, and that "fate" had ordered it so.

It is true that some have been "called home" by sudden death. This was the case with the Prophet Joseph Smith and his brother Hyrum. They had finished their work and the keys of authority, by divine revelation, had been lawfully bestowed upon the twelve. Joseph and Hyrum were in the vigor of their manhood, but the time had come for them to lay down their lives, for it was decreed in the heavens that their passing from this world should be by martyrdom. They had to seal their testimony with their blood and make that testimony binding upon an unbelieving world.

No one in reason would deny the right of our Eternal Father to call an individual home, should he will it. Nor would he argue that to take a person from the mortal life in his youth or early childhood, would be unjust, because it deprived the individual of the pleasures and sorrows of mortality, and the experiences to be gained here. He may call any person "home" at any time he chooses, whether in infancy, childhood, youth, or old age. We are all subject to the will of our Heavenly Father, but we cannot in truth declare that all the righteous dead were "called home" by divine decree.

Is Euthanasia, or Mercy Killing, Ever Justifiable?

Joseph Fielding Smith

QUESTION: *In our study class the question was raised whether or not there was ever a time when mercy killing would be justifiable? For instance here is an elderly person very ill with a disease which the doctors state cannot be cured. The doctor states that he can prolong the life and thus continue the suffering, but death inevitably would finally result. Would he be justified in taking steps to hasten death and end the physical torment of the patient? If consent was given for the doctor to take such a step to hasten death, would he and those who sanctioned it be guilty and have to answer at the time of the judgment?"*

ANSWER: The answer to this question is a simple one. The taking of life was condemned when Cain slew Abel, and for his dreadful sin Cain was punished far worse than to have been put to death. After Noah and his family came out of the ark, the Lord renewed this commandment and said: "Whoso sheddeth man's blood, by man shall his blood be shed: for in the image of God made he man." (Genesis 9:6.)

Who has the wisdom to say that in case of extreme sickness and suffering, there is ever a time when the hope of recovery is past? There have been cases reported many times of persons who were apparently at the point of death and who were in severe pain, who eventually recovered. The answer to this question in brief is, that to presume that the time has come when the person who is ill cannot recover and it would be justifiable to end the suffering by a

From *Answers to Gospel Questions*, Deseret Book Co., 1963, 4:132-37.

painless death is a presumptuous conclusion. The commandment given to Noah is still in force and will be a part of the divine law as long as mortality endures.

This question of "mercy" killing, or euthanasia, constantly arises in the case of individuals who are in severe pain and afflicted with apparently no hope of recovery. It has also been considered in the case of children who are afflicted with some serious deformity which would make them a burden not only to themselves but also to others all the days of their lives. However, there is the matter of conscience which would haunt those who were guilty so that they would live with a feeling of having committed an offense which is unforgiveable, and it seems that they would have no peace.

The discussions on this question apparently will never cease. In the year 1936, this question of "mercy" deaths was presented in a bill before the British House of Lords. The bill was for the purpose of permitting science to decide whether persons should be granted their desire for painless death and was introduced by Lord Ponsonby, Labor leader. Commenting on this the *Deseret News* gave the following:

"In England as in other countries, recent years have seen a growing movement to legalize 'mercy killings' for incurables. Great Britain's several 'mercy trials' have served to arouse interest in the movement, and for more than a year the Euthanasia Legalization Society, supported by prominent physicians and church leaders, has been campaigning for what is termed 'easy death' in certain cases.

"Since an English doctor confessed to taking the lives of five 'incurables,' doctors and laymen have been debating the right and wrong of ending the suffering of people who are doomed to life-long torture and do not wish to live.

"According to the terms of the bill, under debate in the British Parliament, the law would be operated under a referee, who would be appointed by the Minister of Health. Permission of the referee would be necessary before a life could be taken. The act would be restricted specifically to 'illness involving severe pain or an incurable and fatal character.'

"The petitioner for 'mercy death' would have to be

over 21 years of age, and of sound mind. His application
would have to be in his own writing and witnessed by two
physicians. If granted, the proposed 'easy death' might be
administered only by a specially licensed physician in the
presence of an official witness.

"It appears that civilization has already answered this
question without having realized it. The common conscience of mankind declares it a sin and a crime for any
private person to take the life of another. But it also recog-
nizes that the law, whether it be the will of the king or the
will of the people, is the only human agency that has the
right to take the life of a human being.

"Killing by the state, by an officer of the law, or by a
soldier in battle is the only killing now considered
justifiable and not wrong. Therefore, homicide is blameless
if sanctioned by law. But we still face the Sinai law—Thou
Shalt Not Kill—which in its broad interpretation would
place a ban upon any taking of human life."

While this discussion was going on in relation to the
question of euthanasia in Great Britain, the Salt Lake
Tribune also joined in condemnation of such a principle
and the following is taken from an editorial in that paper of
March 12, 1935:

"The taboo against murder is so strong and deep-seated
in our culture that the question of its rightness or wrongness
seldom comes up for consideration. Unlike the more con-
troversial issues upon which public sentiment is more or
less evenly divided, the universal belief in the justifiability
of murder tends to keep the subject beyond the realm of
controversy.

"When border-line cases arise, however, it becomes not
only a matter of news; it is also the occasion of the grounds
for our belief. Much publicity has, therefore, attached to
the case of the 62-year-old woman in England who deliberately put her imbecile son 'to sleep.' The woman was
tried, convicted, and sentenced to hang for the murder of
her invalid son, whom she had nursed for 30 years. In
response to the widespread demand of the British public,
the home secretary, however, recently reprieved the
woman.

"Many people will justify the act of the well-intentioned old lady on the ground that the painless extermination of a helpless defective is a justifiable, nay humane, act. Such an argument, however, loses sight entirely of the social consequences involved. Under such a precedent, anyone, not merely a parent, might assume the right to decide that a given person—not alone a defective—would be better off dead. In a spirit of vengeance, or with a paranoid belief in his own superior judgment, a person might thus administer a death potion entirely without authority and wholly without justification.

"In a civilization that has achieved a measure of success in compensating for many of nature's deficiencies, and in a society that has only just learned the art of prolonging life, it seems a bit premature to encourage the practice of deliberate killing. Moreover, the question of whether a specific disease or a given defect is incurable is not easy to decide, for it is not always a matter of fact. Even with our present limited knowledge of endocrinology, for instance, many imbeciles such as the one Mrs. Brownhill mercifully put 'to sleep' might be cured, provided, of course, the deficiency is not an inherited one. Many conditions which a few years ago were regarded as incurable are now turning out to be within the range of improvement, if not a cure. Until the discovery of insulin, for instance, diabetes was considered hopeless. Pernicious anemia was, until very recently, likewise regarded fatal. The prognosis for general paralysis of the insane, was everywhere considered poor until an Austrian psychiatrist discovered a treatment which has made it one of the most hopeful of all the various forms of insanity.

"There are cases, we admit, in which it would seem humane to painlessly exterminate a futile life. But the practical question is, 'who shall say?' Public sentiment is apparently not yet ready to allow even a well-trained, high-minded physician to exercise this discretion on such a point.

"Given our limited knowledge and the frailty of human nature it would seem, therefore, that the lives of a few hopeless defectives are not to be weighed against the possible subversive consequences of allowing a parent, or even a 'board of exterminators' to decide such issues of life and death."

Let us remember that the life of every person is in the hands of the Lord. Mortal man has not been given the right to judge whether or not a defective soul should remain or be taken from this mortal life. Neither is it within our province to say when a person has completed his mortal course. No other person ever suffered as intensely as did the Son of God, which suffering, as he said, ". . . caused myself, even God, the greatest of all, to tremble because of pain, and to bleed at every pore, and to suffer both body and spirit—and would that I might not drink the bitter cup, and shrink—Nevertheless, glory be to the Father, and I partook and finished my preparations unto the children of men." (D&C 19:18-19.)

We must come to the conclusion, after a careful consideration of this question, that the conscience of any normal person would trouble that person all the days of mortal life, if guilty of such an act. As far as suffering any penalty is concerned that would be a matter deferred to the final judgment.

The Perfect Resurrection

Joseph Fielding Smith

QUESTION: *What will the state of mankind be at the resurrection? This question was raised when discussing the resurrection of the Savior. He appeared to his disciples with the wounds in his hands, feet, and side. When we come forth in the resurrection, will the earthly scars we get and the deformities remain? If we lose a part of the body, like a hand, arm, or leg, will we be made whole?*

ANSWER: A little sound thinking will reveal to us that it would be inconsistent for our bodies to be raised with all kinds of imperfections. Some men have been burned at the stake for the sake of truth. Some have been beheaded, and others have had their bodies torn asunder; for example, John the Baptist was beheaded and received his resurrection at the time of the resurrection of our Redeemer. It is impossible for us to think of his coming forth from the dead holding his head in his hands; our reason says he was physically complete in the resurrection. He appeared to the Prophet Joseph Smith and Oliver Cowdery with a perfect resurrected body. When we come forth from the dead, our spirits and bodies will be reunited inseparably, never again to be divided, and they will then be assigned to the kingdom to which they belong. All deformities and imperfections will be removed, and the body will conform to the likeness of the spirit, for the Lord revealed that "that which is spiritual" is in "the likeness of that which is temporal; and that which is temporal in the likeness of that

From *Answers to Gospel Questions*, Deseret Book Co., 1957, 1:42-45.

which is spiritual; the spirit of man in the likeness of his person, as also the spirit of the beast, and every other creature which God has created." (D&C 77:2.)

The prophet Amulek has stated the case very clearly in these words:

"Now, there is a death which is called a temporal death; and the death of Christ shall loose the bands of this temporal death. . . .

"The spirit and the body shall be reunited again in its perfect form; both limb and joint shall be restored to its proper frame, even as we now are at this time; and we shall be brought to stand before God, knowing even as we know now, and have a bright recollection of all our guilt.

"Now, the restoration shall come to all, both old and young, both bond and free . . . both the wicked and the righteous; and even there shall not so much as a hair of their heads be lost; but every thing shall be restored to its perfect frame, as it is now, or in the body, and shall be brought and be arraigned before the bar of Christ the Son, and God the Father, and the Holy Spirit, which is one Eternal God, to be judged according to their works, whether they be good or whether they be evil.

"Now, behold, I have spoken unto you concerning the death of the mortal body, and also concerning the resurrection of the mortal body. I say unto you that this mortal body is raised to an immortal body, that is from death, even from the first death unto life, that they can die no more; their spirits uniting with their bodies, never to be divided; thus the whole becoming spiritual and immortal, that they can no more see corruption." (Alma 11:42-45.)

Alma testifies to this same thing speaking of the resurrection of our Lord which will give him power to call forth all of the dead. He says: "Yea, this bringeth about the restoration of those things of which has been spoken by the mouths of the prophets. The soul shall be restored to the body, and the body to the soul; yea, and every limb and joint shall be restored to its body; yea, even a hair of the head shall not be lost; but all things shall be restored to their proper and perfect frame." (Alma 40:22-23.)

We must not judge the resurrection of others by the

resurrection of Jesus Christ. It is true that he appeared to his disciples and invited them to examine the prints of the nails in his hands, his side, and in his feet, but this was a special manifestation to them. We should know that the disciples had failed to understand that he was to rise again, and this manifestation was for their benefit. Thomas was absent, and it was with some difficulty that the other disciples could convince him that the Lord had risen. Thomas was not worse than any other one of the apostles. Perhaps they would have done just what he did had they been absent. The Lord said to them and later to him, "Behold my hands and my feet, that it is I myself: handle me, and see; for a spirit hath not flesh and bones, as ye see me have." (Luke 24:39. See also John 20:27.)

When the Savior comes to the Jews in the hour of their distress, as recorded in the Doctrine and Covenants, he will show them the wounds in his hands and in his feet.

"And then shall the Jews look upon me and say: What are these wounds in thine hands and in thy feet?

"Then shall they know that I am the Lord; for I will say unto them: These wounds are the wounds with which I was wounded in the house of my friends. I am he who was lifted up. I am Jesus that was crucified, I am the Son of God.

"And then shall they weep because of their iniquities; then shall they lament because they persecuted their king." (D&C 45:51-53.)

The prophet Zechariah has also prophesied of the Savior's second coming and his appearance to the Jews when they will flee from their enemies and the Mount of Olives shall cleave in twain making a valley in which they shall seek refuge. At that particular time he will appear and they shall say: "What are these wounds in thine hands? Then shall he answer, Those with which I was wounded in the house of my friends." (Zechariah 13:6.) Then they will mourn, each family apart, because they had rejected their Lord.

It is true that he also showed these wounds to the Nephites when he visited with them with the same purpose in view, to convince them of his identity, and give to them a witness of his suffering. It can hardly be accepted as a fact that these wounds have remained in his hands, side, and feet all through the centuries from the time of his crucifixion and will remain until his second coming, but they will appear to the Jews as a witness against their fathers and their stubbornness in following the teachings of their fathers. After their weeping and mourning they shall be cleansed.

What About Cremation?

Spencer J. Palmer

I personally prefer that the bodies of the departed dead be buried in the earth, in graves, rather than cremated by fire (a practice common among Hindus and Buddhists), or left in sacred "towers of silence" so that the corruptible flesh can be stripped clean by vultures (as advocated by Parsis of Zoroastrianism), or disposed of by other means. I prefer this because I am a western man prejudiced in favor of my own traditions. But from the Latter-day Saint point of view there is more to it than this.

From ancient times, the Lord's people have preferred the practice of burial of the dead. In the scriptures it is the unvarying ideal. This tradition most nearly symbolizes the gospel teachings of death, burial, and resurrection—the atonement of Christ—and of baptism by immersion, as Paul suggests in Romans 6. The bodies of the dead are an essential part of the eternal soul. They are sacred tabernacles of the spirit. Out of respect for the dead, their grave sites should be chosen wisely and should be properly maintained. But I see no justification for Confucian theories of geomancy, for thinking that certain surface configurations (topography) are essential considerations in choosing burial sites of the dead. Neither is there any reason to think that the dead spend their time trying to punish, regulate, or reward their living kin on the basis of how well they care for them at death and after. Graves are not religious shrines. The body is ideally put away in a likeness of its

From *New Era*, July 1972, pp. 34-36.

coming forth from the grave, but the life and personality of the dead is neither in nor hovering about the grave. The spirits of the dead go to a place called paradise, a world of spirits, awaiting the day of resurrection.

I find meaning and satisfaction in Joseph Smith's idyllic view of death and the resurrection once expressed in a funeral address:

"The place where a man is buried is sacred to me. This subject is made mention of in the Book of Mormon and other scriptures. Even to the aborigines of this land, the burying places of their fathers are more sacred than anything else. . . .

"I believe those who have buried their friends here, their condition is enviable. Look at Jacob and Joseph in Egypt, how they required their friends to bury them in the tomb of their fathers. See the expense which attended the embalming and the going up of the great company to the burial.

"It has always been considered a great calamity not to obtain an honorable burial: and one of the greatest curses the ancient prophets could put on any man, was that he should go without a burial.

"I have said, Father, I desire to die here among the Saints. But if this is not Thy will, and I go hence and die, wilt Thou find some kind friend to bring my body back, and gather my friends who have fallen in foreign lands, and bring them up hither, that we may all lie together.

"I will tell you what I want. If tomorrow I shall be called to lie in yonder tomb, in the morning of the resurrection let me strike hands with my father, and cry, 'My father,' and he will say, 'My son, my son,' as soon as the rock rends and before we come out of our graves.

"And may we contemplate these things so? Yes, if we learn how to live and how to die. When we lie down we contemplate how we may rise in the morning. . . .

"Would you think it strange if I relate what I have seen in vision in relation to this interesting theme? . . .

"So plain was the vision, that I actually saw men, before they had ascended from the tomb, as though they were getting up slowly. They took each other by the hand

and said to each other, 'My father, my son, my mother, my daughter, my brother, my sister.' And when the voice calls for the dead to arise, suppose I am laid by the side of my father, what would be the first joy of my heart? To meet my father, my mother, my brother, my sister; and when they are by my side, I embrace them and they me." (*Teachings of the Prophet Joseph Smith,* Deseret Book Co., 1961, pp. 294-96.)

This is the ideal—the perfect pattern of death and resurrection. But, unfortunately, this procedure of death and burial is not always possible for man. Nor, perhaps, is it always desirable. Too many people die violent and horrible deaths. Pilots are shot down and their bodies sometimes waste away in prison camps; human bodies are often mutilated, torn, destroyed, and sometimes entirely obliterated by war or accidents of fire and automobile. Some men are buried at sea and their bodies devoured by marine creatures. Not all bodies, not even all bodies of the righteous and the faithful, can be buried whole, or buried in the earth at all. In parts of Europe and in the southern United States the underground water level is so high that bodies cannot be buried in the earth. Hence they are frequently placed in containers above the earth and sometimes placed on top of one another.

In today's world there are local laws in some countries that prohibit burial and encourage cremation; some metropolitan areas in Asia are so crowded that gravesites are a precious commodity and are outrageously expensive. Funeral and burials are prohibitive in cost to some of the most faithful members of the Church in that part of the world. Hence, although I personally prefer embalming and burial and although it has been the pattern followed by Israel, there appears to be no prohibition against cremation in the scriptures or in the theology of the Church. Certainly there is no doubt but that people whose bodies are destroyed by fire (cremated), as was the case with one of our Korean sisters in a recent hotel disaster, will rise again intact in the resurrection from the dead. The fundamental elements of the bodies of mankind are never lost or allowed to belong to another soul. (See *History of the Church* 5:339.)

These will be restored whole, as Alma has promised.

"Now, this restoration shall come to all, both old and young, both bond and free, both male and female, both the wicked and the righteous; and even there shall not so much as a hair of their heads be lost; but every thing shall be restored to its perfect frame, as it is now, or in the body. . . ." (Alma 11:44.)

All of us need to realize that there are Latter-day Saints around the world who prefer cremation to burial. Here, for example, is the view of a young Japanese Latter-day Saint, a returned missionary who is now at BYU, a top student and respected Church member.

"In Japan we often cremate the remains of our dead and I definitely feel that this practice is cleaner than burying someone's dead body under the ground. After cremation only dust and some small bones remain. But just imagine the decay of dead bodies that people put under the ground for the worms and bacteria to eventually take care of. That seems very unclean to me. It is probably a matter of how I was raised. But after the spirit is gone, the body is lifeless material. This material will come back in the resurrection no matter whether you cremate it or bury it underground. So far as Church doctrines are concerned, I don't see anything wrong with cremation. I would rather see cleanliness for the living than sentimental feeling for the dead."

Also, I feel there are unusual circumstances when cremation is preferable and in accordance with the mind and the will of the Lord. The experience of my mission president some twenty years ago in connection with the death of Mark Johnson Vest, an Indian member of the Cocoapas tribe, is a vivid and memorable example in point.

Brother Vest was branch president over an active group of Latter-day Saints at the time of his death. En route to Brother Vest's funeral in Arizona the mission president prayed earnestly that the Lord would tell him why Brother Vest had been taken. As he prayed, he visualized Mark Johnson Vest standing in front of a large group of Indians, which he estimated to be about ten thousand. Mark was preaching the gospel to them. As he did so, one of the Indians in the middle of the group stood up and said, "Do not listen to this man. He is not a Lamanite. He is a Nephite!" After this, Mark Johnson Vest rose to his full stature and said, "I am not a Nephite! I am a Lamanite, and when I died I was cremated according to the custom of my people."

When the mission president arrived at the town where the funeral was to be held, the stake president told him of a serious problem that had developed. Mark's tribe, the Cocoapas, wanted him cremated according to their ancient customs. His wife's tribe wanted him "properly buried." The Cocoapas had said that if he were buried, they would dig him up so they could cremate him.

In his funeral talk the mission president related the vision he had had during the night. This settled the problem of cremation to the satisfaction of both tribes, and there was no more fighting among them over the matter. After the funeral service the mission president and his wife witnessed the cremation of Mark Johnson Vest.

Index